SECRET SOFTWARE

Making the Most of Computer Resources for Data Protection, Information Recovery, Forensic Examination, Crime Investigation and More

Paladin Press · Boulder, Colorado

Also by Norbert Zaenglein:

Disk Detective: Secrets You Must Know to Recover
Information from a Computer

*Secret Software: Making the Most of Computer Resources
for Data Protection, Information Recovery, Forensic
Examination, Crime Investigation and More*
by Norbert Zaenglein

Copyright © 2000 by Norbert Zaenglein

ISBN 1-58160-088-7
Printed in the United States of America

Published by Paladin Press, a division of
Paladin Enterprises, Inc.
Gunbarrel Tech Center
7077 Winchester Circle
Boulder, Colorado 80301 USA
+1.303.443.7250

Direct inquiries and/or orders to the above address.

PALADIN, PALADIN PRESS, and the "horse head" design
are trademarks belonging to Paladin Enterprises and
registered in United States Patent and Trademark Office.

Visit our Web site at www.paladin-press.com

TABLE OF
CONTENTS

WARNING

T he objective of this book is to offer a general overview of the subject of computer resources relating to a variety of applications, including computer security, information recovery, forensic examination, investigation, data protection, and computer crime. Specifically, it is designed to provide those who have little computer experience—from law enforcement officers and private detectives to parents and teachers to business managers—with an understanding of the kind of computer resources available and an overview of their uses.

Increasingly, a wide variety of hacking resources is available to anyone over the Internet. To bring the secrets of these kinds of resources into the mainstream, this book includes examples of procedures performed on the author's computer using software that can be downloaded. Remember, the techniques outlined in this book are for general educational purposes only and *do not* constitute procedures for conducting any computer investigation, especially a forensic computer investigation. An actual forensic investigation must be done by trained individuals using clearly defined procedures that are not outlined in this book.

WARNING

The reader should also note that due to the variation in computer setups, user configurations, operating systems, software, and user preference settings, the examples in this book may not apply to all computers. Here is an example. On most computers, drive "a" is a designated floppy disk drive. A computer user, however, can change disk drive assignments and make drive "a" the hard drive. As a result, an action performed on drive "a" will instead be performed on the hard disk. The act of formatting drive "a" would therefore format the hard disk, with subsequent loss of information. Such a scenario may be unlikely, but it is entirely possible. Keep this in mind when studying the examples outlined in this book.

The reader should not assume, and the author does not imply, that the software referenced in this book is specifically designed for, or is suitable for, investigative purposes or even for the purposes demonstrated in this book. To determine the suitability and appropriate use of *any software*, including the software referenced in this book, the reader must refer to the original software manual or contact the software manufacturer for details.

The examples in this book were performed using specific versions of software on computers running under DOS 6.2, Windows 95, and Windows 3.1. The software, the configurations, the disk drive assignments, the operating systems, and the locations of files and folders and the preference settings on other computers may be different from the examples in this book. Therefore, the procedures outlined in this book may not apply to other computers. The reader is cautioned to consult original software manuals for specific instructions for performing any data recovery procedures, including those outlined in this book.

This book is not intended to be a substitute for the expertise of a trained data investigator or forensic data recovery expert. Nor is this book intended to serve as a step-by-step procedural guide for conducting any kind of computer investigation, computer protection, or safeguarding. The actual procedures must never be performed on the original computer or on an original disk or storage medium. Any computer investigation or data protection procedure must be performed by a trained professional.

Do not perform *any* data recovery, investigative procedure, or data protection procedure outlined in this book unless you do so on a dedicated computer that contains absolutely no useful data or information. Individuals wishing to practice *any* data recovery, computer protection, or investigative exercises, including those outlined in this book, must do so only at a training institution such as a technical college or university, and then only with the advice, guidance, and consent of a qualified instructor. Always refer to specific software manuals and computer manuals for directions on how to conduct any procedures, including the data recovery, data protection, and investigative procedures outlined in this book.

Failure to follow directions outlined in specific hardware and software manuals or failure to consult a data recovery expert or forensic data investigation professional prior to performing any data recovery or investigative exercises, including those outlined in this book, may result in overwriting/deleting information, modifying date and time stamps, compromising evidence, or deleting some or all of the information on a computer.

Furthermore, the improper or illegal investigating of computers might make the evidence gained from such an investigation inadmissible in a court of law.

Always seek the advice of a forensic data recovery expert and legal counsel before performing any computer investigation, data recovery exercises, or investigative techniques. Illegal searches, seizures, illegal data recovery/investigative procedures, or the invasion of another person's privacy may subject the person, the investigator, or the investigative agency to litigation and/or criminal prosecution.

Downloading and using hacking or credit-card generating software to defraud anyone is against the law. The examples in this book are *for academic study only.*

PREFACE

Today's information world seems to have been divided into those who have advanced computer skills and expertise and those who do not. Numerous computer books have been written by experts for other experts. The Web is full of resources aimed at network administrators and other information specialists. Bookstores are stocked with fat books that go into highly technical details. Few books have been written for the common person who does not spend a lifetime dabbling in the bits and bytes of computers to find out what makes computers tick.

This book was written so that novice computer users can understand the issues related to computer investigation, data protection, and data recovery. We now live in an information age; information is a coveted and valuable commodity. Because information is stored electronically, learning how to find, recover, and safeguard it is of paramount importance. We would not leave a valuable ring unprotected, but too often we don't take measures to safeguard and protect the information entrusted to us. Neither do others safeguard and protect private information we have entrusted to them. Your doctor, lawyer, and accountant have private information about you stored on computers. Will these professionals safeguard your privacy? Most do not. Most do not even know that they are giving away personal information about you. In fact, *you* may unknowingly be giving away personal information about yourself and your family.

The amount of information that is available about you in electronic form is staggering. Virtually your entire personal life exists as little bits and bytes on hundreds of computers. You no longer have any idea who has information about you and what they are doing with it.

This book will examine many of the issues related to computer privacy. These issues will be explained in nontechnical terms as much as possible. I'll address some of the software that can be used to protect confidential material and software that can ferret out information. I'll discuss how to find out what is being said about you or your business.

I hope that this book will raise awareness of these important issues.

CHAPTER 1

ELECTRONIC DOCUMENT SHREDDERS

ur personal computers (PCs) have become our electronic confidantes, privy to the most intimate details of our lives. In many ways, computers are like diaries in which we record all kinds of information about our personal and business lives. Computers can record private thoughts that were once conveyed through an e-mail message, or they can store confidential business matters, accounting information, proprietary business records, and any other information concerning our lives.

Our PCs also keep a detailed history of our computer use and our online activity, including the dates and times that particular files and documents were opened, which Internet sites were visited and when, and even our e-mail correspondence. Computers can also permanently store words we entered into the Internet's many search engines, carefully logging these activities.

Equally important is the fact that it is not just our own computers that store detailed information about us. The computer in your doctor's office records information about doctor's visits, medications, and medical conditions. Information about you and any legal disputes you are involved in are stored on the computer in your attorney's office. Your accountant keeps records of your business, tax, and financial information.

Most computer users are unaware of just how much information is recorded and stored on PCs. Furthermore, they don't realize how difficult it is to delete such information permanently. Deleted files, emptied Recycle Bin files, and portions of overwritten files can often be recovered, as is outlined in *Disk Detective* (available from Paladin Press at http://www.paladin-press.com).

The fact that computer history and deleted files can be recovered is of interest to private investigators, law enforcement officers, business owners, managers, and all law-abiding citizens. Why, you might wonder, should law-abiding citizens be concerned with the information stored on their computers? After all, if someone does not have anything to hide, why worry? The reasons for concern are compelling. Let's say you recently consulted an attorney, an accountant, or a physician. Maybe you are going through a divorce, maybe you're about to purchase a business, maybe you have a medical condition. Chances are that your attorney, your accountant, or your doctor will record the details of your visit on a computer.

Suppose you are going through a divorce. The attorney takes notes about your visit and gives these to a secretary, who transcribes them on her computer. Your attorney then forwards your case to an associate in a different office. The associate's secretary takes your divorce proceedings and loads them on her computer so she can work on them. She later "erases" the information on the floppy. A week later, she copies a new file to this erased floppy and takes it home. She opens the new file from the floppy and works on it on her home computer. When she is finished, she sends the new file to her office over e-mail and puts the floppy in a stack with others on her desk.

The information from your divorce proceedings is now at the secretary's home. Sure, your file was "erased," but erased files can be recovered, a process that is not all that difficult. Two weeks later, the secretary's daughter needs a floppy disk for a school project. She picks up the disk that contains your "erased" divorce proceedings and takes it to school. From there, the disk is given to a friend who uses it to store a picture file, which will be sent to an out-of-state friend. Now, the floppy disk that still contains your divorce proceedings is on its way to some other state. After exchanging hands several more times, the disk with your divorce proceedings ends up in the hands of some stranger who decides to look at what information is still on the disk. Guess what he'll find? That's right. Chances are good that he will find the original document created by your attorney months earlier—a document thought to have been erased.

This scenario happens all the time. It's not the exception; it's the rule. Floppy disks are often passed from one office to another, from one person to another, from office to home to who knows where . . . all the while carrying information previously stored on the disk.

Furthermore, this scenario is not restricted to floppy disks. How many doctors, lawyers, accountants, or law enforcement agencies have transmitted their complete business records, including depositions, pleadings, confidential correspondence, profit-and-loss statements, and other records, to some stranger who buys a used computer at a flea market? Sure the doctor, lawyer, or accountant erased all the files or maybe even formatted the hard disk. The problem is that this does not prevent the information stored thereon from being recovered.

The ability to recover deleted and partially overwritten files and computer usage history is a boon for investigators—a second chance to recover evidence. For law-abiding citizens, it's a privacy nightmare. In today's information age you no longer have any idea of who has confidential information about you. Businesses that keep records about their clients must understand how to permanently delete information on computers. In addition, people who use computers for lawful purposes have a right to privacy. It's no one's business what private citizens do on their computers.

Formatting disks or deleting files does not prevent information recovery. In fact, when you delete a file all that is really deleted is a bookkeeping notation related to that file. The actual information in that file is not deleted at all. The process of permanently deleting or overwriting files is called wiping, clearing, or scrubbing.

Unlike "deleting" a file, scrubbing a file actually overwrites information in the selected file or disk, thus making the information virtually unrecoverable.

WIPING IN WINDOWS 3.X AND DOS

Change is the one constant in the computer industry. Pick up any magazine or browse through a retailer's showroom, and you will see promotions boasting about the enhanced features, speed, and function of new technology. The race to introduce new software into the market creates a technological feeding frenzy. Yet, despite the proliferation of new software and operating systems, Windows 3.x and DOS continue to be used throughout the world today. Therefore, this chapter includes information on how to permanently delete files created and stored under these vintage operating systems.

If you use Windows 3.x or DOS, you can use one of the most comprehensive over-the-counter security software programs ever made: Norton Utilities for Windows & DOS. Though it is no longer found in retail stores, you may be able to order this vintage version of Norton Utilities from Symantec's Web site at http://www.symantec.com. Do not use Norton Utilities 8 on computers operating under Windows 95/98 or later. Norton Utilities developed a new version specifically for Windows 95/98 and later applications.

Norton's version numbers can be confusing. The older version (number 8) is numerically higher than Norton's new versions (2.0, 3.0, 4.0, etc.) available at the time of this writing. This might confuse inexperienced users, who may mistake version 8 as being a more recent version. This is not the case, at least not at the time of this writing. Refer to Norton Utilities' user manual for complete instructions and operating system compatibility and requirements.

Files deleted in Windows 3.x or DOS can be recovered using undelete features, text editors, or programs such as Power Quest's Lost & Found. Norton Utilities 8 for Windows/DOS is packed with security features, including wipe capabilities that permanently overwrite files so they cannot be recovered by conventional means. Norton Utilities for Windows 3.x or DOS lets the user set wipe configurations that meet the file deletion standards of the U.S. government.

Files wiped with Norton Utilities are permanently overwritten. Once wiped, information recovery is virtually impossible. A wipe can take from a few seconds to many hours, depending on the amount of information to be wiped as well as the number of wipe repeats. It is always a good idea to wipe information more than once.

You can wipe files, free space, or file slack (disk areas where fragments of deleted files can remain) in computers operating under Windows 3.x or DOS with Norton Utilities. Refer to the instruction manual, then select the wipe settings appropriate for your specific needs. Access WIPEINFO from Norton's main screen. You can opt to wipe files, unused slack space, specific drives, unused disk areas, and even an entire disk.

WIPING FILES IN WINDOWS 95/98 AND LATER

Newer versions of Norton Utilities (2.0, 3.0, etc.) for Windows 95/98 include several security features, but none like Norton's vintage program. Wipe features in more recent versions of Norton Utilities were merged into Norton's Speed Disk utility. Speed Disk is accessed by

Start/Programs/NortonUtilities/SpeedDisk

Speed Disk is designed to improve disk access and speed up the computer's performance. This is accomplished by analyzing file fragmentation and rearranging files so they can be accessed more quickly. If this sounds confusing, think of it as gathering up all the tools from around your house, garage, and car and arranging them on a pegboard. Essentially, this is what Speed Disk does to your files. It picks up all the file fragments and puts them closer together. After rearranging the files, Speed Disk lets the user clear (wipe) the freed up and unused disk areas. To set this wipe option, open Norton

5

Utilities and select Speed Disk. From the Speed Disk dialog box do the following:

1. Click Properties
2. Click Options
3. Place a check in "Wipe Free Space"

After Speed Disk optimizes files, the free space of the disk will be wiped. This process does offer some security, but it lacks the comprehensive features of a true file deletion/scrub utility. One particular scrub utility specifically designed for law enforcement applications is MicroZap.

MicroZap
MicroZap is a secure file deletion program that meets Department of Defense (DOD) standards. MicroZap includes some of the same features found in the earlier versions of Norton Utilities. Specifically developed for law enforcement agencies, MicroZap erases files along with file slack and unallocated disk space. MicroZap deletes files using a three-step process. First, it writes 0s to all file areas. Next, the program writes 1s to all file space. This process can be repeated up to six times. Finally, the hexadecimal value of F6 is written to all areas, and the operating system's bookkeeping record for the selected file is deleted. At the time of this writing, law enforcement agencies can get a copy of MicroZap free. For details about MicroZap, visit its Web site at http://www.forensics-intl.com.

DiskScrub
Thinking about trading in a computer or selling it at a garage sale? Remember, if you fail to take special precautions, all of the data on the disk can fall into the hands of strangers. DiskScrub is a DOS-based program for deleting all data from an entire disk drive. DiskScrub overwrites all information with 1s and 0s. This operation can be repeated up to seven times and can be programmed to meet U.S. government data

deletion requirements for nonclassified material. Under classified conditions, the physical destruction of disks is mandated. DiskScrub, in other words, is much like MicroZap except that DiskScrub will delete (overwrite) information from an entire disk whereas MicroZap is designed to delete single files and unallocated disk areas. DiskScrub can be ordered on http://www.forensics-intl.com.

M-Sweep Ambient Data Scrubber

M-Sweep was developed for notebook and laptop computers. Since these small computers are vulnerable to a higher incidence of theft, they need additional protection. Currently, the sale of M-Sweep is restricted to government, law enforcement organizations, large law and accounting firms, and corporations with a Fortune 1000 rating. M-Sweep is a DOS-based program designed to eliminate information from file slack, unallocated disk space, and Windows' swap file. M-Sweep can be programmed to overwrite data up to nine times. For details visit http://www.forensics-intl.com.

Mutilate

I use a program called Mutilate. Sale of this program is not restricted to law enforcement or large corporations; anyone can buy it. After all, citizens have the right to safeguard their privacy and have an obligation to safeguard the privacy of their patients and clients.

Mutilate is an easy-to-use program that has drag-and-drop features that permanently erase selected computer files. Mutilate lets you customize various security levels. Designed for Windows 95/98 and Windows NT, Mutilate destroys (or "wipes") confidential files, making them virtually unrecoverable. Mutilate works by overwriting all bits that make up the file(s) with binary 1s and 0s, and, if you so select, can write random patterns. A user can select from three security levels. Mutilate can also be customized to make up to 99 passes.

Files are easily selected for wiping using Mutilate's program interface. The free space wiper is another important feature of Mutilate. This will effectively wipe all of the free and slack space of the disk. The Power Mutilator feature allows users to pick 13 folders

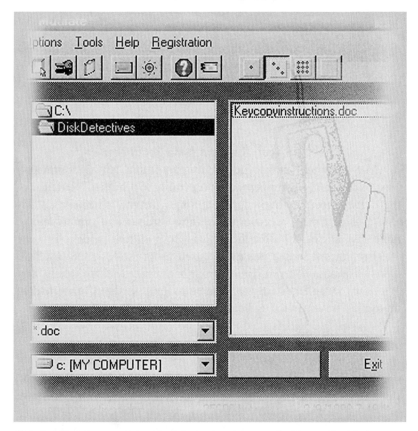

Deleting files does not delete the information they contain. Secure file deletion software prevents deleted information and data in file and disk slack from being recovered.

to access files commonly targeted for routine eliminating, such as the history of online activities.

Other Options and Considerations

Another program you may wish to check out is Complete Delete. Like Mutilate, this program meets the suggested deletion and security standards of the DOD. Norton's Your Eyes Only also includes file deletion features.

You may find file deletion utilities in over-the-counter software such as McAfee's PGP (Pretty Good Privacy). PGP is designed to keep files, folders, and e-mail confidential with virtually impossible-to-break 128-bit encryption. Part of McAfee's PGP software includes wipe capabilities for permanently overwriting information in selected files. If you aren't cognizant of the importance of reading and understanding user manuals, consider the fact that at the time of this writing, deleting a Windows shortcut with McAfee's wipe feature reportedly deletes the entire application. The lesson here is to be careful, read the manual, and know what you are doing.

Another reason to be knowledgeable about wipe procedures is that computer data is not just stored in the files that are created by you. The computer creates its own files in which information is stored. Therefore, even if you wipe a file, a copy of that file may still exist on other areas of the disk. The Windows swap file is one such example. The swap file acts as an addition of the computer's random access memory. When the operating system runs out of memory, the Windows swap file is used as a storage medium. A lot of information, comprising files and fragments, can be written to the swap file, including log-on information, passwords, word processing documents, e-mail information, and Internet history. The Windows swap file can grow to an enormous size and can retain an immense amount of previous computer activity.

In addition to being stored in the swap file (C:/win386.swp), computer activity can be stored and recorded in temporary files, backup files, and other disk storage areas, including the registry. This information can still be recovered long after the original file is deleted, scrubbed, or wiped. History of Internet activity, for example, can be stored in numerous files. Internet Explorer 4, for example, keeps online browsing records in files such as:

- C:/Windows/Cookies/index.dat
- C:/Windows/History/index.dat
- C:/Windows/Tempor~1/index.dat

9

Netscape also keeps track of browsing activity and habits. Some of the files affected may be stored in the following:

- C:/Program Files/Netscape/Users/default/netscape.hst
- C:/Program Files/Netscape/Users/default/prefs.js
- C:/Program Files/Netscape/Users/default/Cache
- C:/Program Files/Netscape/Users/default/cookies.txt

Online browsing information can also be stored in user.dat and related files. Remember, the files referenced above are only examples; your browser may create different files. While some files can be deleted or modified, others cannot. A computer security specialist can suggest ways to remove these files or modify settings and preferences in your system to avoid the recording and subsequent disclosure of information. This can include disabling the history, cache, and cookie files as well as modifying specific registry folders. Some of these files can be deleted or modified without adverse consequences, others cannot. Do not modify, delete, or disable these files, especially in the registry. This can be fatal to your system. Only a computer specialist should perform any of these procedures. You may also ask your computer specialist about a swap file wiper. Since the swap file cannot be accessed in a Windows session, it will need to be deleted in DOS. A subsequent chapter explores software tools that can help protect online and browsing privacy.

As computer usage increases, the importance of wipe and scrub utilities will become more defined. Law enforcement will become aware of where and how to find evidence, law-abiding citizens will be able to safeguard their privacy, and professionals will be able to safeguard the privacy of their patients and clients.

Remember, permanently deleting (overwriting) information requires special software. Careful readers may have noticed that I often use the qualifier "virtually" when referring to the deletion of files using file deletion software. This qualifier is necessary because advanced data recovery techniques might still be able to recover information, even from files wiped with special utilities.

These are extreme measures but can be done. Advanced data recovery works by searching the disk for latent magnetic traces. Analyzing latent magnetic traces requires special equipment; it's not something found at your neighborhood computer store. Searching for magnetic traces is similar to firearm serial number recovery techniques. A suspect can file down the serial number of a firearm so that it is no longer visible. However, the process of stamping the serial number into the gun makes invisible changes to metal below the visible imprint. Using sophisticated techniques, a filed-down serial number can be recovered by analyzing the metal beneath the serial number. Similarly, using latent magnetic trace analysis, even wiped data can still be recovered. This is the reason some government agencies mandate the physical destruction of disks that contain classified material.

If you have specific security concerns or requirements, contact a professional who can advise you as to which software and procedures are right for you. Always read and refer to the user manual and read all precautionary statements. Remember that once files are securely deleted or once disks are wiped, for all practical purposes, this information will cease to exist.

If you want additional information and resources, type the name of the program (or the subject matter) that interests you into any of the Internet's search engines. This way you will get up-to-date information.

File recovery and preventing file recovery are important considerations for law enforcement, business professionals, and citizens. An enormous amount of personal information is stored on our own computers and on computers belonging to professionals with whom we consult. Doctors, lawyers, accountants, and every business that keeps information about its clients must understand wipe procedures in order to maintain the confidentiality of its clients.

The next chapter explores another privacy issue in today's electronic communications world: protecting your privacy through encryption and anonymity.

CHAPTER 2

E-MAIL ENCRYPTION AND ANONYMITY

The number of people who send and receive e-mail is astonishing. It is estimated that more than 40 million e-mail messages are sent each day. That number is expected to increase dramatically over time. E-mail is a quick and convenient way to communicate across town or across the world. Sending or receiving e-mail, however, raises unprecedented privacy issues for businesses, law enforcement, government, and citizens.

Individuals, employees of businesses, military personnel, law enforcement officers, and government employees freely communicate via e-mail, sometimes communicating classified information, private files, or confidential data. Lawyers send confidential documents to other attorneys. People share personal thoughts in e-mail. Police departments share information with other departments, divisions, district attorneys, and prosecutors. Lovers may send romantic or erotic messages or photographs.

Most people never consider the privacy implications associated with sending or receiving electronic mail. The fact is that any electronic correspondence, including e-mail, can be intercepted, monitored, or even modified by strangers. Further privacy implications result from the fact that e-mail is often routinely stored by Internet service providers. This means that not only can your communications be intercepted, monitored, or changed, but permanent records of your communications are in the hands of complete strangers who can access them anytime. It is quite possible that every e-mail message you have ever sent (or received) is still stored somewhere. Remember, unlike ordinary mail, e-mail has to be stored on a server before being delivered (downloaded) by the recipient. That server, or e-mail provider, makes routine backup and archive copies of all the information stored on its computers. These copies can be kept for years or decades. This is why every e-mail message you have ever sent probably still exists somewhere and you have no idea where it is stored or who still has access to it.

What makes e-mail even more vulnerable is that hundreds of thousands of messages can be searched in a matter of seconds for "key" words, by subject, by sender, by recipient, or by any other criteria. That capability makes it a snap to locate and trace specific messages based on any number of parameters.

E-mail can also be compromised by employees of Internet service providers (ISPs) who have access to e-mail messages. While the vast majority of employees who work at these providers are honest and dedicated, their ranks can be seeded or subject to social engineering tactics in order to disclose information. I suspect that curiosity by ISP and e-mail providers also drives prying eyes into e-mail messages.

In a recent survey, 82 percent of survey respondents said they were concerned that their e-mail was being read by others. There is obviously a great deal of concern with sending electronic correspondence.

The threat to e-mail does not come from an Orwellian government conspiracy or supercomputer. No single big brother is monitoring your every message. There is, however, a very real chance that your e-mail can be intercepted, monitored, or read by complete strangers. The lesson is that unless you take special precautions you can never be sure that your e-mail or file attachments are private. E-mail poses both privacy risks and investigative opportunities.

E-MAIL: CAN YOU ERASE IT?

Programs such as Netscape download your e-mail into a mail folder on your computer's hard disk. The location of Netscape's mail folder on my computer is accessed by:

Start/Programs/Windows/Explorer/ProgramFiles/
Netscape/Navigator/Mail

Name	Size	Type
Inbox	424KB	File
Inbox	12KB	SNM File
Popstate	1KB	DAT File
Sent	678KB	File
Sent	20KB	SNM File
Trash	18KB	File
Trash	1KB	SNM File

This illustration shows the location of mail folders in the Windows Explorer. Clicking on Inbox, Sent, or Trash folders opens the corresponding mail folder and allows one to recover previous e-mail even without a logon password.

Here you will find Netscape's three mail folders: Inbox, Sent, and Trash. Each of these folders retains current, sent, or deleted e-mail messages. Anyone with access to your computer can double click one of these mail folders and read these mail messages. In fact, you actually get more information by accessing the mail folder in this manner than over the conventional means (logging on to the Internet). Accessing e-mail through the Windows Explorer reveals the header of the message that reveals the origin of the message along with other sending information. You do not need to know a user's password to access e-mail in this manner. If, for some reason, these files do not open, a file viewer (discussed in a later chapter) will provide access to these e-mail messages.

A novice may try to erase confidential e-mail from his/her computer in one of several ways, none of which are practical or particularly effective. One way is to try to delete one or all of the mail folders. This is not very effective since the Windows operating system sends deleted files to the Recycle Bin. One could empty the Recycle Bin, but information deleted from the Recycle Bin can still be recovered with undelete utilities, disk editors, disk search, or forensic utilities.

Another way to obliterate e-mail is to use a wipe utility. This will permanently overwrite messages, making them unrecoverable. Yet this alternative may be impractical. Deleting or wiping each e-mail message can be time-consuming, and e-mail information will no longer be available for later reference. Individuals frequently need to refer back to previous e-mail messages.

A more practical solution to the e-mail privacy issue is to use encryption software like McAfee's PGP personal privacy software. PGP stands for Pretty Good Privacy.

Actually, with a 128-bit encryption standard used by government and corporations, PGP is more than pretty good; in fact, it's damn good. For all practical applications, PGP works extremely well, though it is not totally bulletproof, especially when used on one's own system. To prevent unauthorized users from reading your e-mail, however, it's an exceptional program.

PGP

PGP is an excellent way to encrypt information. PGP was developed by Phil Zimmerman with the idea of bringing strong encryption to everyone. Unlike conventional encryption systems, PGP uses a dual-key system—one private, the other public. This system avoids the shortcomings associated with single-key encryption. When PGP first appeared, it was difficult to use. Newer Windows versions, however, have become much more user-friendly. Noncommercial (freeware) versions of PGP can be downloaded from MIT, which distributes PGP Freeware for personal, noncommercial use. MIT's site is located at http://web.mit.edu/network/pgp.html. Commercial ver-

Encryption systems such as PGP (Pretty Good Privacy) are an excellent way to protect e-mail, though encryption systems are not bulletproof.

sions are available at http://www.pgp.com. The commercial version has additional security capabilities, such as wipe features.

After PGP is installed on your system, it will generate a public and private key pair, and you will need to provide a password for your private key. This key is then used to decrypt messages. During the installation, PGP also develops a "key ring" that organizes and tracks the public keys you receive from other individuals. The next step is to exchange public keys with those individuals with whom you wish to communicate. You then encrypt and send messages using other individuals' public keys. Your incoming messages are decrypted with your own private key. PGP can also be used to encrypt complete files before they are sent over e-mail.

PGP lets law-abiding citizens protect their privacy and allows for the exchange of proprietary and classified information via the Internet. The downside of PGP is that it allows criminal activity to take place, such as the exchange of classified and illegal material; effectively blocking access to that information by intelligence and law enforcement agencies. To counter this new threat, a number of governments are considering banning encryption or proposing "key escrows" in which encryption keys would be entrusted to third parties. This system would allow governments and law enforcement agencies to effectively break the encryption scheme.

The integrity of any encryption system depends on the proper selection of passwords. To avoid dictionary attacks, never use common words, personal names, or personal information such as Social Security numbers or addresses. Instead, use a nonsensical passphrase that is at least eight characters in length. To remember your passphrase, consider basing it on a personal catchy phrase such as Last Summer I Caught 5 Fish At Lake Tahoe. This phrase would translate to the passphrase LSIC5FALT.

Despite their obvious strengths, encryption schemes can be compromised. Keystroke monitors can capture all keystrokes, including encryption keys. Boot sector stealth viruses can be installed and programmed to activate at the moment the PGP key is used. Recently, a program called PGPCrak was written to expose the lack of security associated with the Windows operating system and the PC. While the program is no longer available, the idea was to show that PGP, in spite of its much-touted security, was indeed vulnerable to a qualified attacker. For all practical purposes, however, PGP is an excellent way to protect confidential information once it leaves your computer. You do, however, need to realize that on your own computer, any encryption keys may be vulnerable.

Another candidate for protecting the privacy of e-mail is Norton Secret Stuff. This software works by creating self-decrypting executable files that can be sent to anyone. What's nice about this is that the receiver does not need a copy of Secret Stuff in order to open the decrypted file; all that's needed is the password, which you provide. Secret Stuff can handle up to 2,000 files at a time. Unlike some encryption programs, Secret Stuff can be exported outside the United States and Canada. This way you can send and receive encrypted files with others around the world.

The use of encryption by private citizens poses problems for law enforcement and intelligence agencies. We live in an age where threats of terrorism are a growing concern. Computers have given citizens access to information about how to construct lethal weapons, including chemical weapons, biological weapons, and explosives, as well as the means to share this information with conspirators. There is also no shortage of individuals and groups who want to express themselves by causing the death and destruction of as many people as they can.

The ability of citizens (or terrorists) to encrypt information blocks law enforcement agencies from information or evidence that could threaten a school, a federal building, or national security. Because of this threat, the government once tried to develop its own encryption scheme that had a built-in "back door" that would have allowed law enforcement agencies to peek at encrypted information after, of course, the appropriate search warrants were issued. The government's plan encountered much resistance and ultimately failed. At the time of this writing, powerful encryption software is available to anyone. Encryption is like a bank vault, it keeps most people out, but anyone determined enough might be able to break in anyway.

Another vulnerability of encryption is that many programs make automatic backups of opened files. If someone were to decrypt a message and open (or edit) it in a program like Microsoft Word, or print it, the security of that message could be compromised. This breach happens because many programs make temporary backups of documents. Printing a file can also leave a copy of the printed document on the disk.

ANONYMOUS E-MAIL

A final e-mail consideration relates to the anonymity of e-mail. A standard-issue e-mail message contains a block of information in the header of the message. The header is usually not visible when the body of the message is opened. The header may include information such as the sender's e-mail address, the name of the originating server, as well as the date and time the message was sent. If you have ever used e-mail, you know that it is easy to determine who sent you the message. Read the message and hit "reply." This brings up a new window with the sender's e-mail address already filled in.

Today, anyone can use anonymous remailers to send anonymous e-mail. Hacker sites often have software that strips the sender's address from the message. Using anonymous e-mail adds a level of privacy to e-mail or to a posted newsgroup message. Once a message is passed through a remailer, the name and e-mail address of the sender are stripped from the message. The message then gets a fictitious e-mail address. Anonymous e-mail has legitimate uses. For example, you might have knowledge of a crime and do not want to give your name to law enforcement. Maybe you know of a major drug or gang activity. Maybe you want to blow the whistle on a government agency that is wasting the taxpayer's money. With anonymous e-mail, you can protect your anonymity while still making law enforcement or others aware of the problem.

You can also use commercial anonymous e-mailers. These companies offer secret accounts that are compatible with most popular e-mail software such as Outlook Express, Eudora, and others. After you sign up with one of these anonymous e-mailers, you can send or receive e-mail to and from an anonymous account. The server strips the headers from all e-mail. To learn more about anonymous e-mail service or to find out more information about this subject, enter "anonymous e-mail" into any search engine's query box.

Your e-mail address, along with personal information such as your age, sex, interests, hobbies, income, and so on, is coveted information. Lots of people want your e-mail address so they can use it for marketing purposes. Online marketers have become very adept at convincing you to give them this kind of private information in exchange for a chance to win something. With this information in hand, they can target zillions of customers with amazing e-mail offers. Once they know your "hot buttons" (e.g., sex, age, hobbies, interests, etc.), they will clog your e-mail with countless offers that seem to appeal just to you. Companies can also get your e-mail address by stealing it, often without your knowing it. This can occur in any number of ways, such as when you download information from an FTP site. Don't think that because your username is "anonymous" that all of your other information remains private. These "anonymous" servers will uncover your real identity, since your e-mail address can be sent to them as the password.

Internet sites you visit can also snatch your e-mail address when you sign a guest book, when you request additional information, or when you fill out forms in contests. Bulk e-mailers now have the ability to pick up e-mail addresses from Usenet newsgroups. After "parsing" through posted information, they will find out what kind of information you are interested in, your hobbies, and so on. Shortly thereafter, your e-mail will consist of mountains of amazing offers such as how to make millions assembling stealth fighter jets in your garage or become a millionaire overnight by investing in the new monetary unit of Transiencia.

NSCLEAN

If you are concerned about protecting your privacy on the Internet, you may be interested in a program called NSClean. This program is designed for 32-bit versions of Netscape Navigator and Netscape Communicator (IEClean for Internet Explorer is also available). These programs let you see the information that the computer stores about you. You can then modify data so that it cannot be obtained by others without your permission. This information includes your Usenet newsgroup activities, your selected e-mail folders, records of Web site visits (history databases), listings of your URL location window, unwanted "cookies," optional removal of bookmarks, traces of graphics and Web pages from cache files, document listings associated with downloads, as well as activity data from the Windows registry.

Most people, I suspect, would avail themselves of such programs if they were only aware of how much personal information falls into the hands of others.

NSClean also gives you the option of shutting down java and java scripts for additional safety. Remember, you are in control over which of these activities you wish to delete or disable. You can clean some computer activities while leaving others intact. NSClean also deletes remnants of your Internet activity along with all tracking data from Web sites and from Usenet newsgroups.

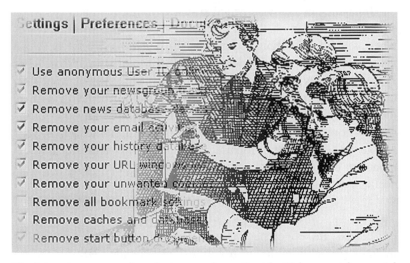

The Internet poses a number of privacy and security risks. Unless you takes special precautions, information about the sites you visited remains on your computer.

EVIDENCE ELIMINATOR

Today's computer user has reasons to be concerned about privacy. Individuals, businesses, and governments have developed powerful tools that can quickly and effectively uncover a computer's history, including online activities, chat discussions, news group postings, sites visited, searches, and more. Furthermore, deleting files, emptying Recycle Bin files, or formatting a disk does not effectively delete that information. In addition, questionable computer activities from temporaries and co-workers who fill in for you can be etched onto your disks. Furthermore, oppressive political systems in many countries make online activities and exchange of information dangerous. Evidence Eliminator can help clean your computer of sensitive information. Evidence Eliminator works below the Windows operating system and destroys unwanted data with methods similar to those used by the U.S. Department of Defense. For more information about

Evidence Eliminator, contact Robin Hood Software at http://www.evidence-eliminator.com.

OTHER SAFETY MEASURES

Another way to keep your e-mail from falling into the hands of e-mailers is to establish more than one e-mail account. Since many services like Excite and Yahoo offer free e-mail, why not set up a junk mail account. Then, you can use one e-mail address for your friends and business associates and another when corresponding with companies you do not know, or companies you might suspect of selling your e-mail address.

There are many legitimate businesses on the Internet. There are also frauds, scams, cons, rip-offs, attacks, and a host of other unsavory offers. Protect yourself on the Internet! Remember, there are numerous businesses doing everything they can to gather information about you, your family, your lifestyle, your hobbies, your interests, and so on. With this information, they establish profiles and demographics about you and your family, which they will use to target you for any number of special offers or amazing opportunities. Profiles about you and your family do not belong in the hands of strangers or marketers. It makes you vulnerable to rip-offs and could compromise the safety of your family.

Think twice before disclosing your income, sex, age, interests, the number and ages of your children, or any other personal information to companies on the Internet. You might even trust the site that asks you to fill in personal information. The problem is that you do not know what happens to this information sometime down the road and who else it will be shared with. Any information you provide can fall into anyone's hands, from a mass marketer to a serial killer. Your personal information is no one's business. We give away too much information about ourselves to strangers by filling out forms on the Internet, tempted by free offers, free information, and chances to win prizes or qualify for other "amazing" opportunities.

Some sites have privacy policies about not transferring information about you to others. Some actually adhere to their stated privacy policies; others do not.

CHAPTER 3

COVERT SURVEILLANCE AND MONITORING

Today's intelligence operatives, law enforcement agencies, and businesses have access to powerful new investigative software that can be put to legitimate uses.

In today's information-sensitive business atmosphere, computer misuse is widespread, and dangers from computer abuse are increasing. With new monitoring tools, today's businesses, parents, and schools can control and minimize computer abuse and prevent losses, fraud, and litigation, not to mention decreased productivity. Security breaches do not just come from strangers; the most severe threats can come from inside your organization, from trusted employees and colleagues. It's a sad state of affairs, but you can't trust anyone completely. If you suspect computer misuse, you can avail yourself of any number of applications that can track who is doing what on your computers.

Keystroke recorders are nothing new. They have been around for years. Vintage keystroke recorders (key traps) secretly record and store every keystroke made on a computer keyboard. This process captures passwords as well as the keys used to encrypt documents, all without the user's knowing that his every move is being recorded. Nothing escapes keystroke recorders—even characters that are later backspaced over are recorded and stored for later analysis. Today, however, an entirely new level of sophistication is transforming keystroke recorders into unprecedented computer monitoring and security resources.

Keystroke recorders can be installed if one has physical access or communications access to a computer. This means that keystroke recorders can be installed remotely; one could be operating on your system right now and you might not know it.

Once installed, the keystroke recorder records and stores all keystrokes in files that can be later examined or transmitted to another computer. Vintage keystroke recorders can be downloaded from hacker sites. Some are freeware, trial, or shareware programs. These programs are usually older and lack the sophistication and capabilities of modern surveillance software. If you are serious about investigation, purchase a commercial software program.

Modern software, like Omniquad's Desktop Surveillance, ushered in an entirely new level of sophistication that gives managers and investigators unprecedented monitoring and control capabilities. Desktop Surveillance can be programmed with recording triggers.

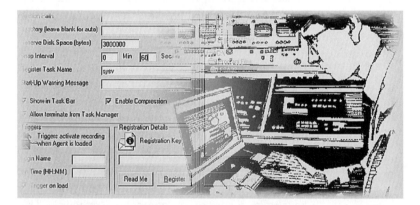

Today, managers and investigators can avail themselves of a new breed of investigative software that can track and monitor computer acitivity, even in real time.

These triggers can activate the computer surveillance at predetermined times or events. For example, Desktop Surveillance can be programmed to be activated at a certain time of the day, or when a selected user logs onto a system.

It can also be triggered when specific Internet sites are visited or when a certain Internet Relay Chat channel is opened. Desktop Surveillance allows investigators to monitor computer activities in real time, over a local network, or over the Internet. Desktop Surveillance can be run in either active mode, as a prevention tool, or in a stealth surveillance mode. The program even stores a visual record of computer activity that can be viewed later, much like a VCR recording.

Desktop Surveillance is the ultimate software for security control and monitoring. The software includes advanced capabilities, such as tracking any of the following:

- Web sites—when they were visited and who visited them
- Who spends the most time playing games or cruising the Internet
- Who tried to uncover other users' passwords
- Who tried to riffle through other files and what they were searching for
- Who edited documents

Another feature of Desktop Surveillance is that it can block access to adult content or to off-limit Web sites, such as hacker or gambling sites. Almost any computer activity can be banned.

Keystroke recorders or advanced monitoring tools like Desktop Surveillance have a number of important investigative applications. A corporation, for example, might suspect one of its employees of transmitting proprietary materials to a competitor via e-mail or in encrypted files.

After consulting with an attorney, the corporation gets permission to install a keystroke recorder on the employee's machine. From that time forward, every keystroke made on that keyboard can be observed or recorded for later analysis. This is one of the keys to unlocking encrypted information. Since keystrokes are not encrypt-

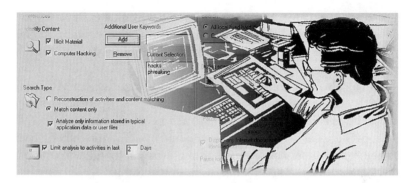

Investigative software can reconstruct and uncover past computer activity by searching for key words, specific file types, and other parameters.

ed, these strokes can be analyzed later to reveal the encryption key. Without the encryption key, it would be virtually impossible for a corporate investigator to unscramble an encrypted message. With a keystroke recorder, however, the encryption key is captured and can be recovered to unlock the encrypted file. With the encryption key identified, the entire encrypted messages can be decrypted.

Omniquad developed another product that may be of interest to readers, especially those with investigative responsibilities. Detective is a state-of-the-art program that can examine past computer activity and reproduce a complete report of computer history. Even material downloaded onto a computer can be retrieved with Detective. With user-defined search features, Detective can detect illicit material and even determine if users tried to delete certain computer activity.

Detective investigates your computer's past and can help determine what it has been used for by reconstructing activities that took place in the past. Several examples of its use spring to mind. A company, for example, might suspect one of its employees of inappropriate or unauthorized use of its computers, such as transmitting proprietary information to a competitor. Alternatively, what would happen if a key employee suddenly died or eloped and you needed to find out what that employee had been working on?

An unparalleled information recovery tool, Detective even identifies when users try to cover their tracks. What makes it so powerful is that it need not have been installed on the computer or network prior to the investigation. In other words, it works backwards in time, bringing previous computer activity into being by analyzing computer history files. Detective's built-in features allow system administrators and others who have valid reasons to access a computer's history to perform investigative tasks that were previously thought to be infeasible.

Keystroke recorders, computer monitoring, and data interception software continue to evolve as security considerations intensify and as operating systems advance in sophistication. One of the most intriguing developments is a program called Data Interception and Remote Transmission, or D.I.R.T. What is both important and alarming about D.I.R.T. is that this program can be surreptitiously embedded on a suspect machine. Furthermore, this embedding does not require physical access to the computer. In other words, D.I.R.T. can be embedded remotely, via telephone. Remote embedding gives law enforcement and intelligence agencies unprecedented capabilities. D.I.R.T. implants itself on the suspect's computer as a hidden appendage to an e-mail message, much like a Trojan Horse virus. Later versions of D.I.R.T. do not even require that an e-mail message be sent; all one needs is the suspect's e-mail address. Once embedded, D.I.R.T. captures all keystrokes. Then, when the computer is used for any online session, the captured keystrokes are transmitted to a control center for investigation.

When a D.I.R.T.-embedded computer is used for an online session, the folks at the D.I.R.T. control center have total access to the computer and all of its resources—all without the computer user's being aware that his every move can be monitored. That may be an advantageous and useful tool for law enforcement. On the other hand, what happens to the privacy of a family member or friend who uses the suspect's computer for legitimate activities? Are his activities monitored and recorded? Is the e-mail he sends to his doctor or lawyer being monitored? These are just the tip of the iceberg in terms of the questions that society needs to address in this new era of investigative possibilities.

Here is a very real scenario in which D.I.R.T. may come in handy: Intelligence agencies learned that a group of international terrorists are planning a biological attack on a U.S. city. Investigators learn that the terrorists are using encrypted e-mail to communicate with associates. After obtaining a search warrant, investigators identify the terrorists' e-mail and surreptitiously embed D.I.R.T. into their computer. The next time the terrorists log on, all of their keystrokes are recorded, including the key used to encrypt and decipher their messages. As agents search for the encryption key, other agents at the D.I.R.T. control center monitor the terrorists' computer and learn of their plans. With enough evidence, law enforcement makes arrests and countless lives are saved.

The terrorist scenario is very real, and the crime-fighting capabilities of keystroke monitors, especially ones that can be remotely embedded, are very powerful. The potential abuses of these programs, however, are enormous. Think about it. Right now, a monitoring program could be embedded on your computer and you would not know it. "But wait," you argue, "I'm a law-abiding citizen living a quiet life in suburbia. Surely I don't have anything to fear from such programs. After all, to search a computer one first has to obtain a search warrant, and besides, I'm an accountant in a candy factory; I've got nothing to hide." So are you safe because you are a law-abiding citizen? Absolutely not!

D.I.R.T. is a powerful investigative tool, and its sale is restricted to law enforcement, military, and government agencies. So why can't you take comfort in the fact that at least the sale of such programs is restricted. Because D.I.R.T. is not the only program on the market. Consider Back Orifice (BO), a program created by the Cult of the Dead Cow. Unlike D.I.R.T., BO is free, available for the downloading from the Cult's site.

BO can be secretly implanted on your computer just like a computer virus. Once installed, it gives a hacker nearly complete control over your computer, all without your knowing that all of your activities are being monitored. Unlike a virus, however, BO was not created to destroy data or cause computer malfunctions. But once it's embedded on a computer, the entire system becomes vulnerable. Anyone on the Internet can access your computer and do almost anything to your system. Even inexperienced hackers can take over your computer, delete files, seize passwords, shut down your system, and so on.

Once BO is implanted on your computer and you are logged on to the Internet, there are individuals actively scanning for you. Finding BO computers is like going fishing. You may not know what fish you will catch, but if you wait long enough, you will catch one.

How serious a threat is BO? Considering that it has been downloaded hundreds of thousands of times, BO can be a serious threat to computer privacy. There are safeguards you can take. Norton Antivirus detected BO after I downloaded the program onto my computer for evaluation. With a little research, you can find a variety of free software on the Internet that can delete BO from your system. One such program is called Back Orifice Eliminator. It is free for the downloading. As its name implies, BO Eliminator searches for and then removes BO from the infected computer. At the time of this writing, there were a number of fixes to BO. But even here, the user has to be careful. Some of the programs that claim to eliminate BO actually implant BO. Be careful. Programs like BO will continue to evolve and advance in sophistication. Information about programs such as BO, how to download them for evaluation, how to determine whether your computer is infected, and how to fix an infected computer is readily available on the Internet. To find this information, just enter "Back Orifice" into any search engine and you will get the latest updates and fixes. Today there are a number of programs that can be surreptitiously loaded onto your computer via a seemingly harmless e-mail attachment. Once installed, they can transmit your data, including online banking information, passwords, and correspondence to an unknown individual.

Another program on the market is the Stealth Keyboard Interceptor Auto Sender (SKIn98AS). This unique software runs invisibly under Windows 95/98 and comes complete with stealth keystroke logging capabilities that save computer keystrokes to a special text file that can be sent to a predetermined e-mail address.

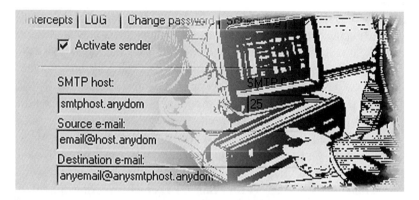

Sophisiticated keyloggers run invisibly and can capture and send all keystrokes to a predetermined e-mail address. This process can transmit all passwords and information before it is encrypted.

SKIn was designed to give the computer user a safety net that records everything typed on a computer for later review or for data recovery. Corporate security personnel or system administrators may find applications for this software in terms of monitoring employee computer activity to prevent abuse, inappropriate computer use, and industrial espionage. Another application might be when parents suspect a child of engaging in inappropriate Internet activity or communicating with a cyber stalker or other predator. Once SKIn is installed, the parents can observe computer activity even while they are working at the office.

You may also monitor computer activities with Spector. Once installed on a target computer, Spector automatically takes a snapshot of visited Web sites, chat room conversations, keystrokes, viewed e-mail, applications run, etc.

With eBlaster installed, you can monitor another computer remotely or have a detailed report of what is taking place on one computer e-mailed to another computer. You can receive reports of Web sites visited, keystrokes typed, programs launched, and screen snapshots. Both Spector and eBlaster are available from SpectorSoft at http://www.spectorsoft.com.

Undoubtedly, programs that spy on other computers will advance in sophistication in the future. These programs will pose significant security concerns for citizens and offer businesses and investigators new means to investigate crime and computer misuse.

NOTE: Monitoring the computer activities of unsuspecting individuals or accessing computers without the permission of the computer user may be against the law. As with all other software outlined in this book, please consult with an attorney before use.

Other software with monitoring and logging capabilities includes the PC Activity Monitor. This general-purpose security tracking software follows and keeps track of all activities performed on a PC, including those performed in a DOS session. Should you keep track of your child's computer or online computer use? Is the cleaning staff using your computer after hours? Do you want to track your own computer use so that you can recover data after a computer crash?

What if you suspect your computer of being monitored by a keystroke recorder? Is there any way to protect your privacy from an unauthorized eavesdropper? With a program called HookProtect, you can detect someone who is trying to invade your computer.

With keyloggers, interceptors, and Trojans so readily available and easy to use, an increasing number of computer users will be subject to computer monitoring without their knowledge. Again, logging devices can be installed surreptitiously while you are away from your computer or while you are on the Internet. Few computer users can detect the installation of such a remote device. Most of these devices are designed to run invisibly. Programs such as HookProtect can detect whether your computer is being compromised or monitored. HookProtect detects keystroke loggers and other monitoring programs that may be active in your computer's memory or on your computer's hard drive. The program works by using heuristic analysis. HookProtect is suitable for use by computer security specialists, system administrators, and individuals working on classified, secret, or sensitive material. A scientist working on a classified project, for example, may install HookProtect to be sure no one is installing a keystroke or other monitoring device. This way, classified and proprietary information remains protected.

PC Security Guard (PC Guard) is another program that can help safeguard your computer against surreptitious monitoring by Back Orifice and other key loggers, interceptors, and spy programs. PC Guard is easy to install and runs after Windows is started.

The only way to stay in touch with the latest developments in this spy vs. spy technology is to update yourself with new information. Install an up-to-date virus checking program and update the definition list frequently. Once individuals become complacent, they fall behind and their systems become vulnerable.

The security, privacy, and law enforcement implications derived from remotely embedded programs and keyloggers are enormous. Suppose that a random sweep with BO by a citizen discovers some kind of illegal activity. That citizen notifies the police. How will this evidence be treated? Will it be admissible in court, or do Internet users have expectations of privacy that would prevent such information from being admissible? If knowledge about programs like BO and keystroke monitoring become commonplace, do we lose the expectation of privacy while on the Internet or while working on computers? Will Internet communications be treated like cellular telephone calls that can be intercepted, or will the Internet be treated like a cable telephone call with expectation of privacy?

The most important considerations for use of any monitoring or recording software are the legal issues. As the laws try to adapt to these new electronic devices, there may be uncertainty about the appropriate use of these devices. Anyone contemplating the use of this kind of software should consult an attorney who is familiar with these issues.

CHAPTER 4

ELECTRONIC
TRUTH SERUM

I magine having a tool that could sniff out if someone you were talking to was not telling the truth. Then imagine if this tool could be used without the knowledge of others. Notwithstanding any legal considerations, such a tool would have enormous potential, and implications, for society.

No matter what business or occupation you are in, the possibilities of such technology are far reaching. The ability to detect lies has unlimited applications: Your spouse calls from the office saying she needs to work late on a special project. You call a number in the classifieds about a used car that's supposed to be in great shape. You are about to go on a first date with a sweet guy you met in the park. You are interviewing someone for a job, or you want to know where your daughter was last night.

In reality, in these and countless other situations, ordinary citizens now have the ability to scrutinize conversations with Truster, the latest voice stress analysis software.

The oldest and most widely recognized truth verification machine is the polygraph. Polygraph tests are administered by trained professionals, and the machines can cost up to $10,000. These machines have been used in the private sector for pre-employment screening and in law enforcement applications. A polygraph examination may last several hours. The polygraph session usually begins with an examination of the equipment followed by a pretest interview. Rubber tubes are placed around the subject's chest and abdomen. Contacts are placed on his fingers, and a blood pressure cuff is wrapped around his arm. The polygraph monitors respiration, changes in the skin's response, and blood pressure/pulse rate. The theory is that as a person lies, blood pressure will rise, heart rate will increase, and the skin will change in response to the electrical current applied to it.

In Truster, the bulky lie detection machines of the past may have a new software rival. A voice stress analyzer that can be operated from just about any modern PC running under Windows 95/98 or later, Truster was developed in Israel for use by the Israeli military. It sifts for the truth by analyzing a person's voice patterns and searching for subtle signs of voice stress that take place when a person lies. Truster's true powers are 1) it is relatively affordable and 2) it can be used surreptitiously, even over the telephone, without anyone's knowledge. NOTE: Some states have licensing requirements that must be met before an individual can use one of these analyzers.

Voice stress analyzers are nothing new; they have been used by police agencies for years. However, voice stress analyzers of old cost thousands of dollars. Now pocket versions are available for $50 to $300. Today, anyone with a computer, Windows 95/98 or later, and a few hundred dollars can put truth verification technology to work. Once installed, Truster can monitor conversations in a room or even over the telephone. Truster offers several modes of truth verification. It can be programmed for on-line monitoring, interview recording and playback, and off-line multiple-participant or single-participant analysis. This unique and controversial software analyzes a person's voice and gives you an on-screen readout indicating whether or not he or she is telling the truth. After a preliminary trial, I felt Truster did, indeed, detect voice stress patterns.

Obviously, Truster raises moral, ethical, and legal issues, as well as questions about how to interpret the results. Anyone who considers using Truster, especially for employment, job terminations, or other such matters, should seek legal advice before doing so. Surreptitiously taping a telephone conversation might be illegal. However, Truster does not record the conversation: it merely monitors it and renders an opinion as to the person's truthfulness.

Since anyone can purchase Truster without having any training in its use, the results should be interpreted cautiously. Even professionally administered polygraphs are subject to misinterpretation and errors. Mistakes can arise from a number of factors, such as improperly placed contacts, poorly phrased questions, equipment malfunctions, or a subject who is truly convinced that he was abducted by space aliens from the planet Zeebouee. Then, of course, one must consider the power of the self-fulfilling prophecy. If the examiner or his employer has a bias, this bias will be reflected in the test results.

The polygraph has its critics, and there are those who doubt Truster's validity. Not surprisingly, one of the most vocal opponents of Truster are the polygraph examiners and the lie-detection industry. Since these individuals have the most to lose from Truster's entry into the marketplace, I treat their assessments with a healthy dose of skepticism, though their camp does raise some valid points.

The typical polygraph examination is conducted by trained examiners who may repeat questions several times. Polygraph results are usually verified before the examiner renders an opinion about the truthfulness

Voice stress analyzers can help detect subtle changes in the voice patterns that can be indicative of lying. As with the lie detector, results are subject to interpretation. Training in voice stress analysis can increase confidence in the results.

of statements given. The polygraph examiner may check the results with one of the new computerized systems, just to be on the safe side. Yet even with such safeguards in place, the polygraph examination is often criticized. Remember, polygraphs measure physiological responses. However, the same physiological responses that accompany lying can occur under any number of other circumstances. Suppose an examiner asks a job applicant if she ever stole anything from an employer. Maybe as a child, the applicant stole a candy bar from a store where her mom worked. Now a deeply religious woman, she had completely forgotten about this event. Now, with tubes and electrodes stretched across her body, she remembers stealing the candy bar and other forgotten memories. She is beset with guilt, embarrassment, and remorse. Will these unrelated recollections cause a response in the polygraph? You bet!

If professionally administered polygraphs are subject to uncer-

A new software makes it possible to monitor the voice stress of individuals over the phone or even from a recording. Remember to adhere to local laws.

tainty, what can be concluded about the findings of inexperienced users of Truster? In my opinion, Truster's role in detecting lies is an adjunctive one.

People use a variety of clues to tell if someone is lying. These might include listening for inconsistencies and watching for nervousness, hesitation, exaggeration, cynicism, closing of the eyes at crucial times, and physical shifting. Any of these behaviors by themselves may not be significant. Someone might be squirming in his chair not because he is lying but because he has an embarrassing itch. By combining a number of factors, however, you might conclude that a person is lying or trying to cover something up. In my opinion, Truster provides one additional factor. Truster's assessment should be used along with other indicators, such as body language, inconsistencies, and so on, before making a truth/lie determination.

Here is another example of how results from Truster may be misinterpreted by an inexperienced user: Your wife calls and says she's working late at the office. You just bought Truster and happened to be trying it out when the call came in. To your surprise, Truster registered a lie. You drive down to the office and she's not there; neither is the boss. Does that mean your wife is at some motel having sex with the boss? Before you jump to conclusions, consider that maybe your sweetie is out shopping for your birthday present for the surprise party she planned this evening. Maybe she went to a male strip show with the girls and didn't want to tell you. Use Truster with care; don't jump to premature conclusions.

We have to remember that Truster is a relatively new program. Over time, Truster and other voice stress analyzers will be refined and will likely evolve into powerful truth verification tools. Undoubtedly, such developments can have an important impact on society. Will we all become better people if everything we say is subject to secret truth verification software, or will we become more reclusive and paranoid? Will government enact legislation to limit or outlaw the use of voice stress analyzers?

TRUSTER BUSTER

This chapter would not be complete without some thoughts about how to defeat Truster. After all, we do have expectations of privacy in our conversations with other people. It's one thing to have the police question a suspect using lie-detection devices; it's another to have your phone call to a friend or employer surreptitiously monitored. The truth is, we have the right to lie if that's what we chose to do. Lying is part of our society. Everyone lies. Doctors, politicians, lawyers, the president, housewives, cops, prosecutors, defense attorneys, priests, teachers, students, spouses, everyone.

Lying can have serious consequences. Lie under oath and you can end up in jail. Lie to your spouse and you may lose your marriage, your house, and your kids. Lying, however, also has important and legitimate uses. Lying can be an important social lubricant. If done with tact and limited to certain occasions, lying helps maintain relations with coworkers, friends, and family and allows us to maintain relationships that would otherwise disintegrate. Would a mother tell her 5-year-old that the breakfast she cooked tasted like something scraped from the bottom of a swamp? No, the mother would eat the breakfast, smile, and lie about how good it tasted. This lie protects her child from embarrassment and from experiencing a sense of failure. Such a lie actually maintains the relationship between mother and child and fosters a sense of self-worth in the child instead of destroying it.

The truth is that our society would not be better off if everyone started telling the stark-naked truth tomorrow. The military would fall apart if recruits told their sergeants where to go, businesses would get sued and lose customers if sales clerks told difficult customers what they really thought of them, and so on.

So can you defeat Truster? I've developed some ideas. Mind you, these are my own formulations; I have not tested them. If you suspect that your telephone conversation may be monitored by Truster or by some voice stress analyzer, you may want to have background noise or music playing. A nice Italian opera with lots of emotional overtones will probably send Truster into a tailspin. Turn on the television or go to where your kids are playing. This would make voice analysis much more difficult. Speak in a low voice or have someone else join the conversation via an extension telephone. If you have a few hundred extra dollars, you may want to invest in one of the voice changers on the market. Voice changers let you modify or change your voice from male to female or anything in between. They are so effective that even your own spouse won't recognize you. My suspicion is that using one will make Truster's job more difficult.

Another trick is that you initiate the call. It is much easier for another individual to monitor your conversation if that individual has had time to set up the software. If you initiate the call, however, he or she may not be ready. If you're paranoid about being monitored you can listen for keyboard taps and the Windows startup jingle. A company called Carl's Electronics sells the plans for an anti-voice stress analyzer. This device lets you pre-process your voice. Once this has been done, it removes all stress. The anti-voice stress analyzer is inserted in the telephone line or between a tape recorder and the microphone. Carl's also sells the plans to a voice stress analyzer.

If you're really concerned, just do it the old fashioned way—put it in writing. As of yet, there is still no way to scrutinize the written word.

BRAIN FINGERPRINTING

Probably one of the most interesting truth verification technologies is brain fingerprinting. This technology is so good it's scary.

Brain fingerprinting works on the basis that our brain waves emit different patterns for a recognized and nonrecognized sound, object, person, and so on. This concept makes sense if you think about it. Things we have seen or heard before are stored in our brains as memory. We have all kinds of neural connections in our brains for our spouse, our mother, our girlfriend, and the like, whereas none exist for a stranger. When we are shown a picture of our spouse, all kinds of memory cells come into play. This activity can be registered

and mapped. Thus, it is possible to determine if we have seen someone before just by monitoring our brain activity.

This ability has myriad applications for law enforcement. For
example, in a murder investigation, a suspect is brought in for ques-
tioning. The suspect denies ever having seen the victim. With brain
fingerprinting, it is now possible to determine if the suspect is lying.

With brain fingerprinting, a series of electrodes are placed on the
suspect's head. The subject is then shown a number of pictures of
people he does not know. In each of these cases, brain wave activity
is normal. Then he is shown a photograph of the murder victim. The
suspect's brain waves register a "murmur" that tells the investigator
the suspect has seen the victim before.

Brain fingerprinting is still in its infancy and will have enormous
implications for investigations. While a suspect may be able to fool
a standard polygraph or Truster, this will not be the case for brain
fingerprinting.

CHAPTER 5

FORENSIC SOFTWARE

ur society is quickly racing into the electronic communications age. Written and published material is increasingly stored as electronic bits and bytes. The ability to exchange information via computer has created new avenues for the criminal element and posed new challenges for law enforcement, business, and government. Today, a number of forensic applications have been specifically designed to access the increasing amount of evidence that may be stored or hidden on computers.

Entering the term *computer forensics* into any Internet search engine will return dozens of vendors. Among these, EnCase has emerged as one of the leaders in the field of computer forensics.

The law enforcement community is increasingly relying on such forensic tools as EnCase to uncover evidence needed for convictions. Evidence gained from a forensically sound computer investigation can put criminals behind bars. Forensic computer searches are uncovering evidence in cases involving child pornography, controlled substances, embezzlement, and fraud, as well as other unlawful activities. Corporations are also discovering the importance of computer forensics in instances involving sexual harassment, wrongful terminations, discrimination, trade secrets, embezzlements, personal injury, and other business situations. In today's computer age, information obtained through computer investigation may ultimately be the determining factor in a court of law. Most computer users don't realize just how much of their past computer activities can remain etched on a computer's disks or other electronic storage media. Using a computer is like walking in the snow. Just as people leave footprints in the snow, computer users leave electronic footprints of their past computer activities. These footprints can remain on computer disks for days, months, years, and even for the entire life of the computer. Visited Internet sites, erased e-mail messages, and deleted files can often be recovered. Even emptied Recycle Bin files can be recovered. Most computer users are unaware of the process that keeps deleted information on the disk. Even the act of printing a file and then deleting and scrubbing the original file can leave the entire document on the disk, waiting to be recovered.

Increasingly, active or "deleted" computer information is the deciding factor in civil and criminal cases. Recovering information from electronic storage media requires forensic tools, training, and expertise. For criminal prosecutions, evidence must be acquired in a controlled manner . . . one that will not change the data on the original storage media. Programs such as EnCase have helped set the industry standard for the forensic acquisition analysis and preservation of computer evidence.

EnCase begins the forensic acquisition by creating a bit-stream mirror image of a target drive. This process in entirely nonintrusive and preserves the integrity of the suspect data. The resultant image that is created is called an EnCase Evidence File. This read-only file or "virtual drive" can be searched and examined in a noninvasive manner. Thus, all original file data, including date and time stamps on a suspect disk, remain unaltered. If disk space is a problem, EnCase includes a compression feature that compacts the evidence file. These compressed files can be

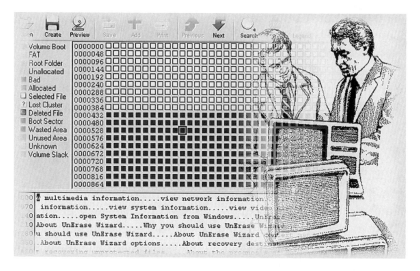

Professional forensics software helps obtain convictions by adhering to forensic protocols.

examined, thus saving space on lab computers.

EnCase also includes a "Remote Preview" feature that allows investigators to observe a target drive remotely using a null-modem parallel (lap-link) cable or through a network interface card (NIC) with transport control protocol/Internet protocol (TCIP/IP). All data on the target hard drive can be viewed and searched at once; there is no need to create an Evidence File. With this process, one can also acquire a target drive remotely through the parallel cable link, or a cross-over network cable.

Today's information is evolving at the speed of thought and forensic applications must constantly adapt to rapidly changing technology. Guidance Software, the developer of EnCase, has a strong commitment to the ongoing development of forensics tools. Guidance Software also offers introductory, intermediary, and advanced computer forensics training courses and provides computer forensic services to assist in criminal investigations and civil litigation support.

For complete information about EnCase, contact Guidance Software at <http://www.EnCase.com> or e-mail info@EnCase.com.

Another leader in the forensic data acquisitions arena is Digital Intelligence. Digital Intelligence develops and manufactures software and hardware solutions to meet the stringent challenges of law enforcement. Digital Intelligence has developed a number of computer systems known as FRED, an acronym for Forensic Recovery of Evidence Device. A generation of FREDs, including FRED Sr., FRED Jr., and FREDDIE (an acronym for Forensic Recovery of Evidence Device Diminutive Interrogation Equipment), can be adapted to a variety of forensic requirements. The convenience of the FRED series is that removed hard drives can be plugged directly into a FRED computer. FREDDIE is a compact system that can be easily carried to a crime scene. Simply remove the hard drive(s) from the target computer and plug them into FREDDIE. For complete applications, specifications, and features, consult the Digital Intelligence Web site at <http://www.digitalintel.com>.

Screen capture courtesy of Guidance Software, the developers of EnCase.

CHAPTER 6

LOCK PICKING THE PC

Many of today's popular software programs have features that allow the user to protect confidential files using electronic locks in the form of passwords. Legitimate investigators, or users who have forgotten their password, need not be blocked from accessing password-protected information. You can find a variety of utilities designed to recover passwords and provide access to the information you need.

Many of today's popular software programs include password protection features. Without the password, entry to the document is blocked. Besides blocking access to password-protected documents, many programs actually encrypt the document, in effect scrambling it so that it is unreadable. Passwords and encryption block access to the information even when disk editors or forensic software are used. Yet passwords can be recovered. The easiest way for investigators to get into password-protected documents is with the help of a professional password recovery program such as that offered by AccessData. You might be able to find free password recovery software and shareware, along with instructions, on the Internet. Searching and finding such software may take a bit of time, and you'll probably end up being connected to a lot of dead links. I have downloaded a number of free programs from hacker sites and put them to the test. Some worked just fine, but I had difficulty getting others to work. Because of the risk of computer viruses and because technology changes quickly, consider spending the money and buying a tested password recovery program such as that offered by AccessData.

There are a number of reasons to have access to password recovery software. First, it is not uncommon for individuals to forget a password. You probably have a number of passwords for a variety of applications. Second, it is not unheard of for an employee to leave a company or die, leaving behind valuable documents protected by passwords. Third, investigators may need to access protected documents when investigating crime or unauthorized computer activity.

The premier password recovery programs for law enforcement, businesses, or individuals who have forgotten their password are available from AccessData Corporation. AccessData has a number of password recovery modules. Personal recovery modules include

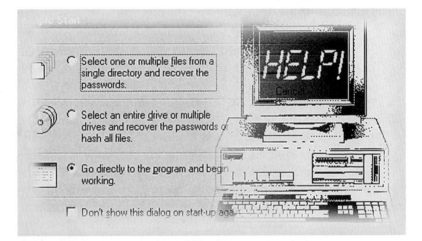

Forgotten passwords can keep individuals and businesses locked out of their documents. Password recovery software provides a measure of safety against forgotten passwords.

- Quicken®
- MS Money®
- Lotus Organizer®
- Ascend®
- Scheduler Plus®

Other password recovery modules available from AccessData at the time of this writing include

- WordPerfect®
- Word®
- Excel®
- Lotus 1-2-3®
- Paradox®
- Q&A®
- Quattro Pro®
- Ami Pro®
- Word Pro®
- MS Access®
- Approach®
- QuickBooks®
- Professional Write®
- DataPerfect®
- ACT®

Network Utilities including a NetWare access utility and an NT access utility are also available.

The password recovery software is supported with free technical support and a user manual on the CD. AccessData's password recovery modules can be ordered as individual units or can be purchased as a complete toolkit. Advanced features include dictionary capabilities, as well as the tools to set up a biographical profile. A trial version of the program is available at the company's Web site at the time of this writing.

Another supplier of password recovery software for a number of programs is CRAK software.

INTERNET LOG-ON PASSWORDS

Suppose investigators need to find someone's log-on password in order to read unread e-mail messages. Remember, some e-mail messages are not downloaded onto the computer. If you recall, earlier we discussed how to access e-mail that is stored in folders on the computer. In some instances, e-mail is not downloaded onto a user's computer but remains on the server. Unless you have the log-on name and password, you won't be able to retrieve the e-mail messages.

Recovering e-mail messages may be useful in a missing person investigation where a minor corresponded with an adult. Unread e-mail messages may reveal plans, motives, or interests that can lead investigators to coconspirators, accomplices, or individuals with knowledge of someone's whereabouts.

Recovering log-on passwords is based on the fact that other computer components, like modems, must process log-on information and passwords. While the software that connects the user to the Internet may encrypt the password, the software that drives the modem may not. Therefore, searching other computer files can uncover e-mail log-on names and passwords. Assuming it is legal, here is an approach that is somewhat complicated and time consuming but may work.

Assume you need to find a log-on password for Netscape running under Navix. You may not be able to find this information in the Netscape files or folders, but you may be able to extract it from other files. Here is how this can be done:

1. On a different computer, set up the identical Internet, mail, and browser software. Set up a new Internet and mail account (including a unique log-on name and a very unique password such as hickorydickorydockery).
2. Use your new Internet setup to log on to the account you established.
3. Log off.
4. Use a program such as Expert Witness to search the entire disk for the log-on password you created (hickorydickorydockery).

5. Note the file and location and surrounding information of where you found hickorydickorydockery.
6. Search the original computer (a duplicate in a criminal investigation) in the identical location, and you may discover the original user's log-on name and password.

Because of the large number and variety of browsers, Internet access software, and modems, there may be no easy way to recover log-on names and passwords. Hackers often use social engineering tactics (befriending someone who works for the Internet service provider) to get information. Others use pretexts to get an unsuspecting employee to release password information.

Many people sign up for free e-mail accounts through companies like Yahoo. When you set up a free account, you will usually be asked for some key information that identifies you. For instance, you might be asked to create a question and answer that identifies you, such as "What is your mother's maiden name?" or "What are the last four digits of your Social Security number?" The answers are the key that releases the password. Thus, you may be able to get someone's password by finding out what the answer to the question is. Parents who suspect a minor of corresponding with a predatory adult may not encounter any legal problems in doing this. Otherwise, those who use such procedures open themselves up to civil and criminal repercussions.

CHAPTER 7

SPY GLASSES FOR YOUR PC

FILE VIEWERS

No investigator's toolkit should be without a serious file viewer like QuickView Plus or KeyView Pro, just to mention a couple. Suppose you come across an e-mail message or a file that can't be opened.

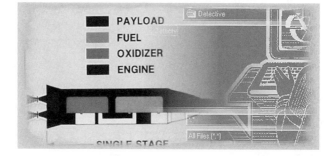

File viewers allow individuals to view a variety of documents, even if they do not have the software application for that file.

It happens all the time. Maybe the software required to open the file has been deleted from the computer or someone sends you an e-mail with a file attachment for which you do not have the software. In either case, having a file viewer will give you instant access to the information you need.

File viewers let you see and print database files, embedded graphics, spreadsheets, video clips, recorded messages, pictures, compressed files, e-mail, Mac material, and others. It's like having hundreds of software applications on your computer.

PRINT SCREEN UTILITIES

In the prehistoric days of computers, users had a great little button on their keyboard known as the Print Screen. If you look on your keyboard, the Print Screen button is still there. In the days of old, you could click this button and your printer would print out whatever was on the computer screen. With the advent of Windows, this nice feature somehow fell into oblivion. Today, however, you can recapture the use of the Print Screen button with instant print software. I use Instant Print Screen, a basic and affordable program.

Print screen software gives you a printed copy of anything on the screen.

Suppose you are examining an exact duplicate of a floppy disk and want a printed copy of what's on your computer screen. Having a print screen utility makes a printed copy just one click away.

LANGUAGE TRANSLATORS

Today's world is becoming a global community. Visiting other countries and cultures is just a click away on the Internet. Our communities comprise people who speak different languages. Therefore, it is not uncommon to discover information in any number of foreign languages. Police officers, hospitals, and emergency medical personnel may encounter people on the street who do not speak English. Maybe they are just passing through town when an emergency strikes.

Translation software brings the world into your computer.

Years of intense linguistic evaluation combined with recent advances in computer technology and artificial intelligence made possible these advanced language translation features. In the past, it would have been time-consuming and expensive for an investigator to handle foreign language documents. Today, language translators open the door to the world. I use Universal Translator, which, at the time of this writing, translates, types, and even spell-checks 33 languages.

This futuristic technology uses artificial intelligence to translate documents between different languages, e.g., English to Japanese, Vietnamese to English, or any one of 1,000 different language pair combinations.

Many online services now allow for language translation. Although language translation programs are not perfect, they can provide valuable glimpses into information that would otherwise be inaccessible.

CHAPTER 8

DETECTING
AND IDENTIFYING
INTRUDERS

How do you know if someone is trying to break into your computer? As a reader of this book, you obviously have an interest in securing your computer and protecting information from prying eyes and malicious programs. One unsettling fact is that the next time you cruise the Internet or send an e-mail, someone could be monitoring your every move, retrieving your confidential files, or destroying valuable data.

Special software will let you know if intruders are trying to break into your computer.

InternetALERT '99, from BONZI Software, lets you determine whether someone is trying to break into your computer. InternetALERT '99

A protected computer can even generate a map of the intruder's physical location.

allows you to map the intruder's ISP contact information. This allows you to report the attack to the intruder's ISP or set up an "attack log" that includes the intruder's IP address and port number, as well as the date and time of the attack.

You will also get a map of the intruder's ISP location. Today, a growing number of individuals and employees, including attorneys and law enforcement officers, use computers for business and online activity, from research to e-mail to data transfer and so on. Practicing secure browsing is no longer a luxury. With so much at stake, can you afford to open your computer to hackers or hostile programs that can jeopardize your information? The browser you are using may have some safeguards, but can it protect you against different attacks? If you are concerned with your computer's security while online, you may wish to evaluate a program such as InternetALERT '99.

CHAPTER 9

STEGANOGRAPHY AND ENCRYPTION

The use of personal computers is skyrocketing, and computer users frequently store personal, confidential, and proprietary information electronically.

Another trend that makes information more vulnerable is the increasing use of notebooks and laptop computers. These smaller computers are common targets for theft; not only is your hardware gone, so is all of your proprietary information.

Steganography is the process of hiding one file inside another. Steganography can keep confidential information from prying eyes.

A text document can be encrypted and hidden inside a picture file, giving no visual clues as to its existence.

It is also not uncommon for a number of users to share the same computer. Having read this book, you know that few computer secrets are safe from prying eyes. Anyone with physical access to your computer or who is clever enough to embed a remote transmission device onto your computer can access all of your information.

The need for securing confidential information has never been greater than it is today. If you want to protect confidential information, you may want to look into security encryption software such as Norton Your Eyes Only. This software lets you protect files with on-the-fly encryption for folders and directories you specify. Norton encrypts documents using RC4, DES, triple DES, and Blowfish. Once encrypted, these documents are virtually impossible for anyone else to read. Several other features include the BootLock feature, which gives you boot-up access control, and ScreenLock, which locks the computer screen after the computer has been idle.

Another commonly used tactic is to hide your files within existing graphics, sound, text, and even HTML files. Here is where Steganos packs a double punch. This software first encrypts files, and then it hides the encrypted file within an existing file.

When you use only encryption, your data may be unreadable, but it is obvious that there is sensitive data there. This could allow someone to take further action to try to recover that information. If, however, your data is encrypted and hidden, it will be extremely difficult for anyone to find this information. Because it does both, Steganos is an excellent way to safeguard information from others. As we have seen, computer security can be enhanced by steganography and encryption. The software that accomplishes these tasks is often affordable, and using it adds a measure of privacy and security to your electronic documents when you share a computer, work on sensitive documents, or store confidential information on a laptop that can be easily stolen.

CHAPTER 10

UNDERCOVER AGENTS ON THE 'NET

Information on the Internet is increasing exponentially. Today, information about virtually everyone is on the Internet. However, your name, address, telephone number, e-mail address, and so forth, are not stored in databases that are accessible to anyone.

Finding information about you or about people, places, and subjects of interest can be a challenge. The Web poses significant security and privacy risks for companies and citizens alike. So much information is available on the Internet that we have to wonder what is being said and stored about us. This concern applies not only to businesses but also to individuals. You would be surprised to learn just what kind of information can be found about you on the Web. Credit report headers, your address, your telephone number, driving directions to your house, your neighbors and their telephone numbers, and what property you own are just a few examples.

WHO'S TALKING ABOUT YOU AND WHAT ARE THEY SAYING?

As Web-based information increases, it will become critical for businesses and citizens to find out what information about them is being openly circulated on the Internet. A business, for example, may want to know who is using their trademarks or copyrights or who is chatting about them and what they are saying in newsgroups. What companies have linked to your Web site—or to your competitors'? Who has stolen your files?

A program called Who's Talking is a complete investigative package wrapped up in a high-speed, multi-threading "spider" that speeds through the Web to find specific information being said in newsgroups and in other selected areas. This program was originally developed to ferret out unofficial use of company trademarks, copyrights, and so on but has many uses beyond this capability.

I downloaded a trial version of Who's Talking and put it to the test. The results were i m p r e s s i v e . Running through each of the five searches proved easy and effective. First, I tried an HTML search for specific keywords. I

Software that searches the Internet keeps an eye on your reputation by uncovering who is saying what about you.

wanted to see what information I could find about a convenience store homicide in Cozad, Nebraska. After entering the keyword (Cozad), Who's Talking went to work, searching the top 10 search engines. Within a few minutes, Who's Talking uncovered the information I was looking for. The program also returned an impressive number of hits about the town itself.

Next, I ran a newsgroup search. This feature of Who's Talking searches through all major newsgroups for selected keywords. You might be surprised at what you'll find and what others are saying about you, your business, or your products and services. Companies might be interested in who is linking to their site or who is linked to their competitors' sites or to their graphics files or scripts. Since Web pages may not be indexed by all search engines, Who's Talking includes a "Site Search" that lets users search a selected domain. It will then visit and follow links and directories, searching for your keywords. Who's Talking outputs search results in a controllable database that can be exported in a number of formats, including HTML.

OTHER SPY UTILITIES

You once had to be part of a privileged group of investigators to access private information about people or companies. With so much information on the Web today, it can be challenging to find the information you need. Knowing where to look will help you in your search for information.

One of the products I put to the test is a program called the Cyber Detective Toolkit. This software was easy to install and easy to use.

With Cyber Detective, you can find out virtually everything about someone or about his or her business. Programs like Cyber Detective are used by private investigators to locate online sources for conducting background checks and employment checks or tracking and locating people. Cyber Detective provides a quick link to these and other investigative resources on the Internet, many of which are free. You can, for example, search for someone's e-mail address, physical address, and telephone number, and even get a map to their home. Other resources, however, require credit card payments before they divulge private information.

The Cyber Detective Toolkit also provides quick links to adoption resources, Social Security databases, military databases, investigative sources, bankruptcy filings, lawsuits, criminal records, tax liens, state government resources, and state-by-state information including government databases and court documents.

The Cyber Detective Toolkit also includes a variety of snoop utilities. These utilities can help parents or employers monitor online activities. While not a forensic program, this software makes an excellent training tool for law enforcement officers who want to

With investigative software, the Internet's vast information resources are just a click away.

familiarize themselves with the Internet and with basic computer investigative techniques.

Cyber Detective's Disk Snoop feature lets you search the computer for Internet files such as graphics, text, and HTML files. Cyber Track is a monitoring utility that can be used from a floppy. Once installed, it monitors and tracks Internet activity. The Cyber Detective search utility consists of a small icon that will load in your system tray. When it's activated, you can find people, newsgroups, and businesses, as well as conduct general searches.

A final feature is the Investigator's Electronic Notebook. This lets you organize your caseloads in information searches with a daily planner, a contact and investigative source database, case logs, and a missing persons checklist. For my money, the Cyber Detective Toolkit is well worth it.

Another contender for conducting Internet investigation is the PI Web Browser. The PI Web Browser is not just a set of bookmarks; it is a browser that you can use, like Netscape and Explorer. At the time of this writing, version 7.0 was just released. This program features a new tool that allows you to search the Web for any keyword. A finger tool lets you search for e-mail addresses. The WHOIS tool lets you determine the owner of a particular Web site. The PI Web Browser lets you search for people, their addresses, and their telephone numbers and even do reverse telephone lookups. In order for the PI Web Browser to work, it must have a PPP or SLIP connection. If you don't know if you have one of these connections, you can contact your e-mail provider.

A third contender is Cyber Spy Toolkit. Cyber Spy is an HTML-based toolkit that uses hyperlink menus and frames to access information previously in the realm of private eyes. With just a few clicks you can track down a skip trace or be connected to reverse directories, look up a Social Security number, and locate underground online resources. Also included are links to investigation databases, public records, military records, motor vehicle records, missing persons and adoptee databases, newsgroup searches, and more. You can also track down information from newspapers around the globe, locate people who have changed their names, access military databases, and create maps directly to a person's address.

This comprehensive toolkit also has links to illegal drug archives and the ability to retrace anyone's newsgroup posting. From databases to driver's license records to criminal records, this program has many useful links. At the time of this writing, it cost around $20.

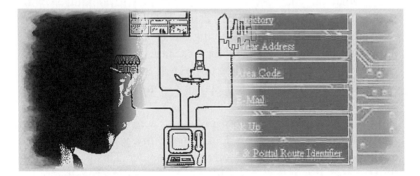

Savvy investigators are turning to the Internet to uncover the information they need.

All of these programs are well worth the investment, especially for individuals who are not that familiar with online navigating and information resources. Remember, while some information links are free, others will require payment to access information. You can spend a lot of money online. I suppose it's worth it if you do get the information you need. I suggest you log on to the Web sites of the various software and learn which one is right for you and your budget.

MORE INVESTIGATIVE TOOLS

PI Scan is a program designed to work with Windows 3.1, Windows 95, Windows 98, and Windows NT computers. The information is gathered from a floppy that is run through Windows. PI Scan exposes the following files on a hard disk or network drive:

- Web pages
- Gif graphic file names
- Jpeg graphic file names
- All other file names

Since this program needs to be run in the Windows environment, it may not be suitable for forensic purposes.

A variety of software programs can help you uncover who's doing what on your computer and what they're looking at while online. Employers, for example, can find out if their employees are visiting porn sites, online gambling sites, or sports sites. Among a number of software contenders for these tasks is the CIBIR Computer Scanner. This program searches for HTML, gif, or jpg files.

A program called Triple Exposure scans the computer for pictures, videos, and keywords.

Computers store a history of online activities. There are two ways to find out who's been doing what. First, you can learn where and how to access these files on your computer. This can take a little expertise. If you lack this skill, you can invest in a search tool like Triple Exposure, which tracks inappropriate computer use. Triple

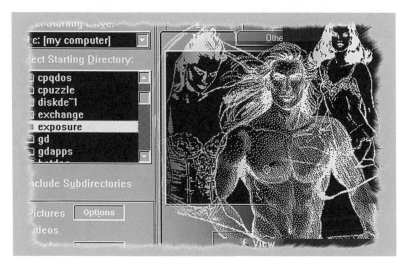

Locating and identifying inappropriate material can be a challenge for parents and teachers.

Exposure is not a filtering program. Despite their usefulness, filtering programs can be disabled, and they may not filter out all unacceptable sites. In addition, filtering may lock out information to appropriate resources.

Parents, schools, or employers can use Triple Exposure to search for and identify inappropriate material, like visits to hacker sites or sites that feature pornographic material. Letting someone know that their computer use is being monitored will act as a deterrent to inappropriate activity.

CHAPTER 11

IMAGE ENHANCEMENT

S ecurity cameras will forever change the way we live and work. Surveillance cameras are everywhere. Miniaturization accompanied by low prices spurred a dramatic increase in visual electronic eavesdropping. Today, anyone can buy a coin-size video camera and install it anywhere they want to. Cameras and transmitters are frequently disguised as household items: a radio, a VCR, a teddy bear, a smoke detector, a table lamp, a fountain pen, or a pager, just to mention a few. Any ordinary object can be a video camera. You can no longer take your privacy for granted, no matter where you are or what you do.

Like other human endeavors, video cameras have both a negative and a beneficial role in our society. Surveillance cameras can identify criminals, solve crimes, monitor employee activity, and reduce shoplifting losses. They also provide a powerful deterrent to crime. After all, the goal of the criminal is perpetrate the crime and then slink surreptitiously back into the night with the spoils of his plunder. Knowing that a crime can be captured on video is likely to make him think twice. Likewise, an employee is less likely to raid the company cash register when someone is watching. A shopper is less likely to steal when he or she knows store security is staring down from the ceiling. However, not all criminals are deterred by surveillance cameras. Many more don't know they are being recorded.

While crimes are increasingly being captured on video, photo analysis and identification of suspects or license plates can prove difficult. The story is an all too familiar one: A suspect is accused of murder. A security camera captures the act on tape. Yet the images on the videotape are distorted, making it difficult to identify the suspect or specific details of the crime. For a jury to come back with a "guilty" verdict, a clear picture is required, as was seen in the Reginald Denny case in Los Angeles. Helicopters hovering above the 1992 Los Angeles riots captured images of truck driver Reginald Denny being yanked from his truck and beaten into a coma. Defense lawyers relied on the poor quality of the videotape to get their client acquitted. They argued that their client could not be positively identified. However, cops had a new high-tech video enhancement weapon. This powerful image processing technology was developed by Cognitech, Inc., of Pasadena, California. Dr. Rudin of Cognitech testified as an expert witness in the case. On July 5, 1996, a California Court of Appeals determined that Cognitech's technique was "sufficiently established to have gained general acceptance in the field." Cognitech's Video Investigator is based on the application of nonlinear differential equations. Analysis of the tape focused on a black mark on one of the attacker's arms. Video analysis determined that this mark matched a tattoo on the suspect's arm. The attacker was convicted thanks to the video, but more so to the enhancement of the video.

Low light, poor video quality, accumulated dirt, and electronic noise can distort images, making it difficult to identify suspects or license plates. The FBI, Secret Service, and other intelligence agencies borrowed technology developed by NASA to enhance these electronic images and put criminals behind bars.

Technology once in the purview of intelligence agencies has moved onto main street. Anyone with a computer, video capturing software, and a photo image editor can do a pretty good job of enhancing images.

In the real world, many law enforcement agencies operate on exceedingly tight budgets and are in no financial position to purchase high-end software that they may use once or twice. Due to cost factors and a learning curve, many investigators rely on commercial photo enhancement software, often with good success.

QUICK IMAGE ENHANCEMENT

Shoplifting and other minor crimes captured on video do not justify spending thousands of dollars on a forensic image enhancement software program. But for a few hundred dollars, most people can do a good job clarifying a video or photographic image. Computers are increasingly equipped with digital interfaces, yet the capture of video frames can require the installation of hardware such as Zip Shot. Once installed, Zip Shot can turn motion video into high-quality still images that can be analyzed. Once an image is digitized, you can make and distribute thousands of copies. While not specifically designed with forensic applications in mind, such image capturing devices, in my opinion, have applications for law enforcement or civil cases where cost is a factor.

Zip Shot lets you capture and digitize clips from just about any video source. After capture, these digitized clips can be reviewed, analyzed, saved, printed, or saved as AVI files. Zip Shot, for example, supports domestic and international video standards including NTSC, PAL, SECAM, and S-Video.

Images can also be enhanced using image enhancement software. This process can significantly sharpen the image and reveal details not visible during normal video play or while glancing over a printed photograph. The details captured could make the difference between a conviction or an acquittal.

Interfaces like Zip Shot capture video images in resolutions up to 1600 x 1200 pixels.

The image at right is an actual still photograph of a video clip of the car driven by a suspect in a convenience store homicide in Cozad, Nebraska. Note how no portion of the license plate number is readable.

This particular image was captured from a Web site and subsequently subjected to basic image enhancement using low-end photo enhancement software.

First, the license plate was cropped from the rest of the image. Next, the plate was enlarged. Hue and saturation of the color image were adjusted. Converting the image to black and white seemed to provide more clarity, and subsequent analysis was performed in black and white. Different adjustments of sharpening, brightness, contrast, highlights, midtones, and shadow seemed to offer some clarification of the plate. Turning the image into a negative also improved clarity.

After some analysis, marks that resembled the letters YID seemed to emerge.

Looking closely at the letters in the lower side of the frame seems to reveal marks resembling the letters YID.

Yet, what appeared to be letters raised a number of puzzling questions.

First, these letters seemed to line up in a straight line, while the license plate of the suspect's vehicle was at a slight angle, presumably from the position at which the camera was mounted. How can you reconcile what appears to be letters in a straight line with a license plate that is at an angle?

The second question had to do with the relative sharpness of the letters YID against the blurred license plate. Why would these letters be so sharp when the rest of the license plate was blurred?

The only logical conclusion was that something else made these characters. I don't know what made them, but it is likely that these characters were not made by the suspect's vehicle. If you're disappointed in this analysis, you shouldn't be; in fact, it's damn impressive if you think about it.

Photograph in reverse also seemed to reveal marks resembling the letters YID.

- First, the analysis of this photograph was made from a picture snatched off the Internet; it was not even an original video image. Who knows which generation photograph this was, or how it was processed, captured, uploaded, or handled?
- Second, the image analysis was performed using the basic functions of an elementary photo-editing program.
- Third, the original license plate image was extremely small, measuring a diminutive .16 x .31 inches.

Taking these factors into account, it is quite remarkable to pick up what appears to be markings left on such a small image, even if they turned out not to be the license plate numbers. Performing additional analysis of the photos did reveal several important new clues that were misidentified in the original investigation.

I refocused on the photographs snatched from the Internet. After cropping away irrelevant material, I filtered the images and zoomed in. When I did this, I found that the original description of the suspect was in serious error. The suspect was described as wearing

Note the dark band around the suspect's waist. This is a belt, meaning the pants are trousers, not sweatpants as was reported. Also note the unique cut and trim at the bottom of this jacket. This suspect was identified as wearing a bomber jacket and sweatshirt. This is by no means a traditional bomber jacket. This is a single garment with a unique double collar that may give the impression of having a sweatshirt beneath it.

sweatpants. Enhancing and zooming in on the image, however, revealed a dark band indicative of a belt.

Further analysis of the photograph revealed other important clues. Mind you, this analysis was performed with nonforensic software by someone who only had basic photo enhancement skills. Even with such simplistic tools, I discovered important details that had been missed by law enforcement.

(As an aside, I contacted the Nebraska Law Enforcement Training Center on several occasions, thinking that surely they would be interested in seeing how technology might be useful in solving crimes. They never acknowledged my letters. It is a sad state of affairs when there is more investigative power in the hands of

Enhancing, zooming in, and analyzing the receding hairline revealed important clues about the suspect's age. Although the suspect was originally described as being in his early 20s or 30s, the receding hairline may be indicative of an individual who is beyond his early 20s. Note the double collar.

ordinary citizens than in law enforcement.)

Having already uncovered new information, I was quite encouraged by the results and decided to pursue this image enhancement further. In the process, I discovered other clues that were missed in the original investigation.

As we have seen, performing image enhancement and studying the image carefully can reveal important details. Enhancing an image does not change the fundamental integrity of the original image. By enhancing I mean adjusting brightness, contrast, hue, saturation, highlight, midtone, shadow, sharpness, and so on, in order to bring out or clarify certain details. This should, of course, be performed on a copy of the image, not on the original.

With video and surveillance camera usage increasing, the applications for image enhancement technology are broad and far-reaching. Law enforcement agencies, private detectives, and company security personnel can all benefit from understanding image enhancement techniques and capabilities. Whenever possible, the image enhancement should be performed by a professional. However, many small law enforcement agencies do not have the financial resources to send the image(s) to a lab for analysis. In that case, there is nothing to lose by conducting image enhancements, as long as the work is performed on a duplicate of the image, not on the original.

FACES: PUTTING IT ALL TOGETHER

After uncovering new details about this case on a home computer, I pushed forward, seeing what else I might be able to uncover using software.

It was difficult to tease out an identifiable image of the suspect from the still photographs on the Internet. Each photograph revealed a different angle of the suspect, and he looked different in each captured image. Making identification more difficult was the fact that the photographs were distorted.

What was needed was a way to study the actual video clips and determine whether a composite picture of the suspect could be created from the video images.

The weight of this suspect was reported at 200 pounds. Compare the size of the suspect's wrist to the "lay" of the sleeve. The sleeve reveals several inches of slack. This is a bulky garment and makes the suspect appear much heavier than he is. I feel the suspect is 20 to 30 pounds lighter than was reported.

One of the captured video images of the suspect in the Cozad homicide. This cool, calm, calculating killer shot a feamle clerk to death a few minutes after this picture was taken. Note the rolled-up pants and bare feet.

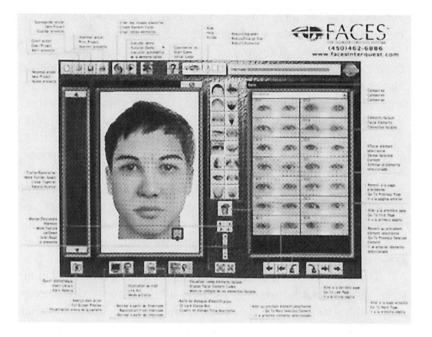

The point-and-click features of FACES software made it easy to create a composite of the suspect.

I obtained a second-generation copy of the video from the Cozad, Nebraska, Police Department and subjected these images to further analysis.

First I needed to capture the video clips and turn them into still images. It took about 15 minutes to hook up the Zip Shot hardware we discussed earlier. Next I installed the video capture software that came with Zip Shot. After hooking up the hardware, I borrowed a new VCR and followed Zip Shot's directions for capturing video images.

About ten minutes later, I had captured the images of the video surveillance and converted them into still images so that they could be analyzed and subjected to basic image enhancement techniques. All original captured images were stored in a separate directory. All enhanced images were stored in their own directory. This way the original images would be retained.

The final piece of the puzzle was to create a composite picture from the captured video images. FACES software was the logical choice. Seen onAmerica's Most Wanted, FACES is the revolutionary software from InterQuest that redefined the way composite pictures are created. I purchased a copy of FACES for $50 and put it to work.

In the past, forensic artists would interview witnesses or victims. Based on witness descriptions, the artist would sketch a composite. Many forensic artists are skilled professionals who create extremely accurate facial representations. The dilemma, however, is that not all law enforcement agencies can afford their services. Smaller agencies or those located in rural communities simply do not have the financial resources to enlist the skills of a forensic artist. FACES software, however, changed all of that.

The software incorporates nearly 4,000 facial features, including eyes, noses, lips, and so on. It includes all the tools needed to construct a remarkable array of facial characteristics. After the facial representation is complete, the composite can be sent across the world in seconds using an alphanumeric identification key called InterCode. FACES, which is very affordable and relatively easy to learn and use, overcomes one of the biggest obstacles in catching the bad guys: the lack of an an accurate description of the criminal that can be released to the public and other law enforcement agencies. Just eight hours after an armed robbery in Lexington, Nebraska, police created a composite picture of their suspect using FACES software. A few hours later, they arrested a suspect. This story is one of many successes credited to FACES software. Since its inception, FACES has helped capture killers, rapists, and pedophiles. In 1998, a spokesperson for a Florida police agency reported that FACES helped nab the south Florida rapist. A Sheffiff's deputy used the software to create a composite, and an arrest followed shortly. On of the more amazing captures using FACES happened in Canton, Michigan. A real estate agent was raped in a model home. She was able to provide a description, but police needed more. The victim herself sat down at the computer and, without any prior skills, used FACES to create a composite of her attacker. Once the composite was released, tips started pouring in. One of the tips came from another real estate agent who was able to supply a driver's license number. A short time later, a suspect was arrested. The composite created by the victim was virtually identical to the suspect. FACES allowed this victim to fight back and catch her attacker. As it turned out, the attacker had spent time in jail for another rape.

With the availability of FACES, law enforcement agencies now have an affordable means to construct quality composites quickly and easily.

While FACES has historically been used to construct composites from victim or witness descriptions, the program seemed highly adaptable to creating a composite from our captured video image. Since different video frames revealed different facial features of the suspect, one could, in theory, construct a composite from analyzing the various images captured from video.

I had never used FACES before. It took only a little practice to learn the program. Flipping between the images I captured and FACES, I started putting the pieces together. The composite picture took several hours to create. Since I was working with a number of captured images, was inexperienced with the software, and constantly enhanced the captured images, the project took some time to complete. After studying the captured video images, enhancing the video captures, identifying suspect characteristics, and using FACES, I pulled together a likeness of the suspect.

The result of this project is represented on the following page.

Please note that any similarity between the surveillance photographs and composite picture shown and any law-abiding citizen is coincidental. All suspects should be considered innocent until proven guilty.

PROFESSIONAL OPTIONS: VIDEO INVESTIGATOR

The fact that I was able to use a home computer with over-the-

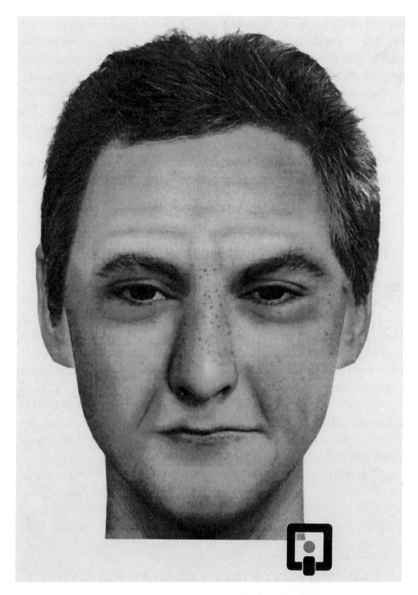

Final suspect composite created after analyzing various video clips.

counter software to identify important new information in an existing homicide case was encouraging. Hopefully this example will serve as a wake-up call to law enforcement agencies that have not yet subscribed to the power of the computer.

Sometimes, producing a high-quality image and extracting as much detail as possible from a video frame is important for investigators and prosecutors. In these cases, a professional video enhancement tool may be indicated. Cognitech's Video Investigator is a comprehensive video analysis program developed to meet the exacting needs of law enforcement agencies. The software has a number of important features, including

- Video restoration capabilities to restore degraded videos and provide the most clarity to an image
- Videogrammetry that collects existing crime scene measurements, which are used to deduce other information, such as the height of a suspect
- Frame fusion, which can combine different frames of a moving object (the license plate of a vehicle leaving a crime scene, for example) to create a clear copy
- Mosaic, which can combine portions of frames and merge them into one picture
- Visualization tools, which can help investigators monitor the sequence of the investigation
- Video cataloging tools, which organize captured video sequences in accordance with content and can be intelligently queried as well as other advanced features

It is clear that Video Investigator is a state-of-the-art program designed for today's exacting forensic requirements.

The image on the following page shows a license plate too dim to be read. After applying frame fusion techniques, the characters of the plate can be identified. Note how even the letters "MONROVIA" are clearly visible. (Some portion of the license plate has been purposely blocked.)

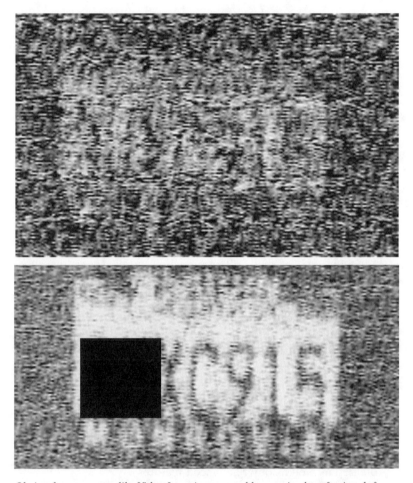

Obviously, a program like Video Investigator, used by a trained professional, far outweighs the capabilities of standard-issue software.

Today's security professionals and law enforcement personnel must have a working understanding of image enhancement techniques. Proper handling and analyzing of videos and other electronic images will lead to accurate crime scene descriptions. The result will be convicting more criminals and exonerating the innocent or wrongfully convicted.

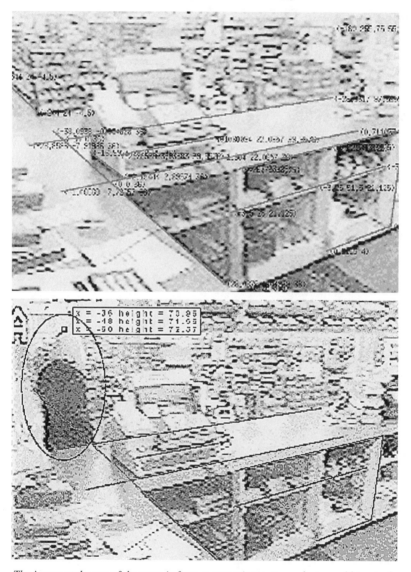

The image at the top of the page is from a convenience store where a robbery took place. Using videogrammetry, measurements are collected from the environment and used to determine the height of the suspect in the photograph above.

CHAPTER 12

SECURITY GUARDS FOR YOUR PC

ALL-IN-ONE PACKAGES

Computer security is always a concern. The data stored on computers is at risk when the user leaves his or her computer unattended, carries a laptop or notebook, or connects to the Internet. I have discussed a variety of security software throughout this book. In this chapter, I'll provide a brief outline of several all-in-one security programs. Many of these are very affordable and provide comprehensive protection against any number of common threats.

PC Security for Windows is a comprehensive program that protects your computer and its files. It includes a number of security features, including Explorer Control, File Lock, System Lock, Shortcut/Program Lock, Restricted System, Windows Lock, Intruder Detection, and Password Protection. PC Security is available from Tripical Software, which also offers a variety of security software, including encryption and keyboard monitoring programs and Private Pix, which allows you to view encrypt picture files so that pictures can remain private while stored on a computer or being sent over the Internet.

Explorer Control offers robust desktop management tools to restrict access to unauthorized individuals. Explorer Control controls the operation of the desktop, start button, control panel, and printers and has features that let the user control a variety of display properties. More important, the System Control lets the user hide drives, disable registry editing tools, and hide desktop items. PC Security also lets the user remove the "Run" or "Shut Down" command, among others.

File Lock blocks user-chosen files by requesting exclusive use of that file from the operating system, thus making the file unavailable to any other user.

System Lock blanks the screen so that not even a mouse or a tap on the keyboard will start the computer. Only the password will unlock the screen. System Lock can be programmed so that it activates upon startup or after a certain amount of inactivity.

Shortcut Program Lock works similarly to File Lock. Instead of blocking files, however, this feature assigns programs to the exclusive use of the operating system. Once this option is set, no one else can use that program.

Restricted System lets the user determine which programs can be operated. Acceptable programs are placed in a Permitted Programs list. Different users can be permitted to access different programs.

Windows Lock locks specific windows. Once locked, these windows will not respond to mouse movements or keystrokes. Users can lock the window by either disabling it or making it invisible.

Intruder Detection alerts you in the event that someone tries to access your computer using passwords. After a defined number of password tries are entered, the system will show the date and time the intruder tried to access the computer and will activate an alarm, lock the desktop, and issue a warning.

Norton's Your Eyes Only can safeguard your information by encrypting and decrypting private files. The software also lets you share files without compromising security. It can lock access to your PC when you step away for a few moments and prevent unauthorized users from booting it. Only authorized users can read the files.

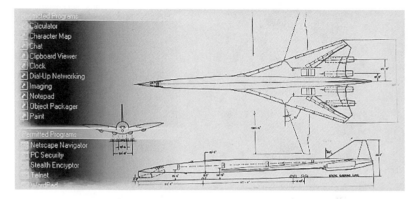

Security software can keep unauthorized personnel from accessing confidential, restricted, and classified information.

As time passes and security concerns increase, additional programs will be developed. For more information, visit your local software outlet or software catalog. Better yet, log on to the Internet and do some searching to find the program that has the security features you want. If you are concerned with security or restricting access to your files, please consult a professional.

CHAPTER 13
TEMPEST

O ne of the most intriguing and little-talked-about technologies of our time relates to a much-guarded secret called TEMPEST. TEMPEST, also known as van Eck monitoring or van Eck eavesdropping, is based on the fact that anyone with the right equipment can sit outside your home, office, or apartment and be able to see what you are doing on your computer, including activity that is on your screen. Right now, a van may be parked across the street. A hidden antenna is aimed at your window. While you are working away on a classified document for your company, a competitor is capturing your every word.

Van Eck technology works by gathering electromagnetic transmissions emitted from your computer equipment. Emissions can come from microchips, monitors, cables, and printers. These transmissions can be picked up from hundreds of yards away and reassembled later into readable information.

Bank, military, government, and business computer systems can be compromised easily because of the radiation emitted from their computer systems. It is even possible to single out a computer from amidst many because each computer emits a specific signature. Data is further compromised by the fact that the computer's disk spins constantly beneath the read/write head. This means that electromagnetic signals can continue to be emitted even though no one is working on the computer.

Some papers have spelled out steps that could be taken to safeguard against escaping emissions. These include installing metal screening or wallpaper, putting the computer inside a metal jacket, or using encryption. Since this type of radiation can leak from many sources, I doubt that these means are completely effective.

One report told of someone using an aged Russian television set that was based on a continuous tuning frequency. Using a makeshift antenna, they reportedly captured screen images from a variety of computers.

TEMPEST is an acronym for Transient Electromagnetic Pulse Standard. This standard is used by the government to measure and determine a safe level of emissions.

As it turns out, electromagnetic waves emitted from computer equipment act much like radio waves. And, as we all know, radio waves can be intercepted.

TEMPEST standards are a closely guarded secret; you can probably understand why the government is concerned about this issue. Having someone sit outside CIA headquarters monitoring the activities taking place inside presents a nightmare problem. Unlike keystroke recorders and other computer monitoring devices, TEMPEST monitoring cannot be detected.

Obviously, such monitoring techniques have severe privacy implications, not only for national security but also for businesses. Most businesses have closely-guarded secrets—trademarks, for example— and are vulnerable to spying from competitors and others. TEMPEST-proof computers are expensive and out of reach for most citizens. For TEMPEST test services and solutions for computer monitors, printers, scanners, laptops, and other systems, consult a professional.

CHAPTER 14

FILE RECOVERY

O ne can imagine any number of nonforensic applications where a data recovery program would come in handy. Suppose an employee leaves a company and accidentally or intentionally erases critical files.

At one time, if your data were lost you would have to spend thousands of dollars to have it recovered by a professional. This process was not only expensive; it was also time consuming. Today, however, you can use software like Lost & Found to recover and restore data after deletion, be it from an accident, from a corrupted file, or from a deliberate act.

Power Quest's Lost & Found can recover data if a particular disk partition was reformatted or if the File Allocation Table (FAT) was destroyed. As long as a disk drive is still running, there is a good chance that Lost & Found can find and recover files on the disk. You don't need to have Lost & Found installed on the computer in order for the program to recover deleted or corrupted files or files lost due to the formatting of a disk.

Lost & Found is being used by some law enforcement departments to recover deleted files.

Obviously, a number of factors come into play when trying to recover information. No software can guarantee full file recovery, but Lost & Found is an excellent utility. Lost & Found works under DOS and may not be suitable for novice users.

CHAPTER 15

HIGH-TECH CRIME AND THE UNDERWORLD OF THE INTERNET

Computer use is skyrocketing, and the Internet is racing into the next millennium at an unprecedented pace. Computers and the Internet will revolutionize the way we live, work, shop, learn, and play. Technology places the world's informational resources at the fingertips of everyone with a keyboard connected to the Internet. Educational institutions can now bring their classrooms directly into the nation's homes. New businesses have flourished as entrepreneurs have set up shop on the information superhighway. Students have discovered new ways to explore the world and communicate. Like all other human endeavors, however, computers and the Internet are a double-edged sword. It didn't take long for the dark side of the Internet to emerge.

Today, the Internet is used for fraud, crime, shams, rackets, sex, gambling, gunrunning, terrorism, espionage, assaults, stalking, and abductions, just to mention a few. A few media reports focused on the Internet following the Columbine High School shootings in Colorado. However, the connection to the Internet probably escaped most people.

I suspect that the majority of adults—parents, teachers, lawmakers, and law enforcement officers—don't fully comprehend the nature or scope of the Internet issue. The laggard pace of the political and legal process is woefully inadequate in a world where technology evolves at the speed of thought.

Can you buy an assault rifle over the Internet? Can you find free hard-core and child pornography? Can you get step-by-step instructions for making homemade explosives or drugs? Can you get fake ID and credit card numbers? Can a minor buy alcohol? Can you obtain fake diplomas and degrees? Can you get computer break-in tools? The answers to all these questions is yes! And while this process might seem difficult to most adults, for most kids it's as easy as buying a can of pop.

Our society is woefully inadequate in handling this situation. To stem the abuses of the Internet, some are calling for censorship. But the call for censorship is misguided. After all, you would not censor all books because some books contained information to which you objected. You would not ban all movies because you found some movie scenes or content objectionable. It's the same with the Internet. Censorship is not the answer.

The issue of the Internet is one of parental oversight and control. Children are impressionable, and it is the responsibility of the parents or guardians to monitor, control, or restrict information accessible to minors. The problem is that too many adults harbor a fundamental lack of understanding about technology, the Internet, and what their kids are exposed to online. This information has been swept under the carpet for too long. Without understanding the issues, you can't monitor or control the problem.

Again, censorship is not the answer. For one thing, it's impossible to censor or control the Internet. The Internet is beyond control. You have to remember that the Internet is worldwide. Local laws have a difficult time dealing with a business operating from overseas. From the standpoint of the Internet, an overseas site is just as close as a site from across the city. Restricting information does not work, and it is dangerous. What does work is parental monitoring of the activities of minors. For parents to monitor and control, they need to understand how the Internet works.

So let's begin our explicit journey into the underworld of the Internet by exploring some of the software available, how it is accessed, and how it can be misused.

PICK A CARD, ANY CARD

Most people, especially adults, will be surprised to learn just how easy it is to generate valid credit card numbers. Anyone with a PC and access to the Internet is only a few minutes away from having the ability to generate hundreds of valid credit card numbers. And that's just the tip of the iceberg in terms of computer crime resources available from a keyboard connected to the Internet.

Dozens of credit-card-generating programs with names like Card

Entering terms such as "hacker cracker" will lead to hacking sites and related hacking and carding material.

Pro, Credit Master, and Credit Probe are free for the picking off the Internet. Credit-card-generating software is normally plucked from various hacker sites. Hacker sites can be found by entering the words "hacker cracker" (see illustration above) into any search engine. To increase the chances of getting credit card or other carding software, enter the term "hacking cracking carding." Doing this and then clicking on "Search" will bring up hundreds of hacker-related sites, each with its own selection of software free for downloading. The hacker sites displayed will depend on which search engine is used. The illustration at the top of page 98 shows a fraction of the results from a "hacker cracker" search entered into the Excite search engine.

Search engines make finding hacking sites easy. The hacking culture is intriguing, and their site offers numerous resources that can be used for academic study.

A variety of carding software is available from hacker sites, some quite sophisticated.

Credit-card-generating software can be misused but may find legitimate uses for law enforcement demonstrations and academic study.

As you can see, cracking programs, including password-generating and credit-card-generating software, are easy to find. Finding hacker sites is simple. The next step is to download the files needed for study. Since many law enforcement officers and other readers are unfamiliar with the process or pitfalls of downloading, we will outline the process here in some detail.

Readers should note that downloading any file from the Internet poses the risk of catching a computer virus. I've downloaded hundreds of files, many from hacker sites, and have never had a problem. You, however, might not be so lucky. Be sure to have a virus protection program installed with updated virus definitions. Even then, you should not be lulled into a sense of complacency. Virus detection programs are not 100-percent foolproof. Independent tests show that some viruses escape detection from the best antivirus software.

Once you've logged onto a hacker site and find a program you want to download, all you do is move the cursor over the underlined (or highlighted) program name and double click. This starts the process of downloading the selected file. After the file finishes downloading, the computer prompts for a directory location of where this file is to be stored. You can select the location by clicking on the arrow in the "Save in" dialog box. After selecting the location, click on "Save" to download the program.

The Vcard program in our example came compressed in ZIP format. In the illustration on the previous page, note that the "File type" has a ZIP extension. Most files plucked off the Internet will be in some kind of a compressed format, like ZIP. This reduces both the file size and downloading time. For the end user, this means having to perform an intermediate step (unzipping) before the file can be used.

There are a number of ZIP utilities that can be purchased for about $30. You can also find and download free and demo versions of UNZIP programs right off the Internet. Enter "FREE ZIP PK ZIP PK UNZIP" into a search engine and look for sites that offer free, demo, or shareware programs. Most downloaded ZIP programs are self-extracting and will, for obvious reasons, not require an unzip program.

After performing a quick search, I was able to locate several sites that offer free ZIP software and demo versions. To avoid the impression of endorsing a product and because many sites are here today, gone tomorrow, this book will not specify any addresses that

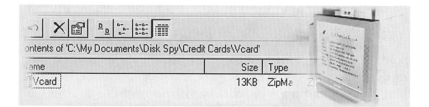

Downloaded software is often compressed (zipped) and must be unzipped (extracted) before it can be installed. Decompression software is inexpensive and sometimes even free on the Internet.

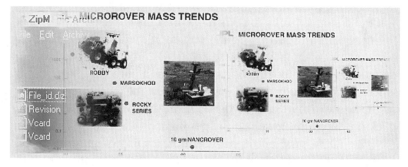

Zipping is a way of compressing data.

offer free software. It's best that individuals studying this subject learn how to find information on their own.

Once a file is downloaded and properly extracted, you will have to learn how to use it. Many downloaded files include the actual program files as well as the instructions on how to use the file. The instructions or manuals that accompany these programs are often quite brief. Inexperienced computer users may have to go through several trial-and-error exercises to get these programs to work. Often, these programs are older versions. Many still operate in DOS; others are fully Windows-compatible.

Part of the illustration on page 101 shows a sophisticated Windows-based credit-card-generating software program. Note how

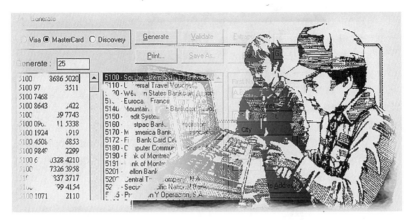

Anyone can access credit-card-generating software and other programs. Adults should monitor children's computer activities.

this program allows the user to generate Visa, MasterCard, or Discover card numbers by clicking on the appropriate category.

The generated cards have, of course, been blocked for obvious reasons. This particular program also lets the user select from a list of bank names, bank identification numbers, and certificates, as well as generating user names and addresses.

Obviously, the credit card numbers generated by programs like the one outlined above will, in all probability, not be active ones. That is, a merchant verifying one of these numbers for the purchase of a $1,000 diamond ring will not get clearance from the bank. But these card numbers can be used to place telephone calls, order online services, gain access into adult sites that require credit cards, and fool unsuspecting merchants.

On the Internet, anyone with about $2,000 can buy a state-of-the-art credit-card-capturing system like the one exposed on a national television news program in 1999. With the accompanying software and hardware, anyone with basic computer skills can rake in thousands of dollars in cash and merchandise by remotely seizing credit card and calling card numbers, along with their PINs, credit limits, and expiration dates.

Magnetic stripe copiers and card reader/writers are also available for anywhere from a few hundred dollars to around $1,500. These machines allow anyone with a laptop and supplied software to change the data stored on the magnetic stripe of credit or calling cards—a neat trick, especially since blank cards are easy to obtain. Take a stolen credit card and swipe it through the machine. The computer will display all of the personal information encoded on the card. This information can then be transferred to a blank credit card. Thus, in a matter of minutes, hundreds of valid credit card numbers can be generated. That's the high end of the credit card fraud game, where the stakes and legal consequences are high.

CYBER SEX

So what happens once your 12-year-old has a credit card number? Well, then you can be sure that he (or she) will try to use it to go somewhere or do something.

Sex seems to be the most popular destination on the Internet. Sex on the Internet can be explained simply: If you can imagine it, it's on the Internet. If you can't imagine it, it's also on the Internet.

If you are a parent, imagine the last thing you would want your child to see. Whatever you've just imagined, it's on the Internet, and it's right at your child's fingertips. Many sites offer free pictures and samples.

While writing this book, I switched my computer over to my Web browser, logged on to a search engine, and typed in the word "sex." Within seconds, a banner popped up showing a woman with enormous breasts spilling out over a black-laced brassiere. The banner beckoned, "Click here to Enlarge." From there, I got a choice of sites to search for, among them Amateur, Celebrity Nudes, Gay, Oral, Fetishes, Gay Men, Swingers and Groups, Free Pictures, and so on.

You get the message. I'm only a click or two of the mouse away from hard-core material. What kind of material? Again, if you can imagine it, it's on the Internet; if you can't imagine it, it's also on the

Internet. There are no taboos. And with a credit card number, it's just moments away—movies, pictures, stories, you name it. The cycle is completed, from finding software to downloading software to generating credit card numbers to using them.

It's really no one's business what consenting adults look at or do in the privacy of their homes. It's none of my business; it's none of the government's business; it's none of the church's business. The problem is that kids should be shielded from this material, and they're not. Parents, schools, and libraries can protect kids from this material by employing some spy software of their own, some of which was discussed in earlier chapters. For the purpose of this chapter, consider installing a program like Cyber Patrol, Net Nanny, Internet Safe, or Disk Tracy. These programs control and block access by children to pornography, cyber-strangers, gambling, bomb and drug formulas, and so forth.

UNDERAGE? NO ID? NO DEGREE? NO PROBLEM!

Besides generating credit cards numbers, computers can be used to create fake identification or order false credentials. The quality of these documents can be good enough to fool experienced law enforcement professionals. Want to disappear, create a new identity, or just get a college degree without taking any classes? It's all available online by entering the search word of the item you are looking for into any of the Internet search engines.

Suppose someone spent his younger years smoking pot and collecting welfare. Now he's sobered up and wants to get a job. The problem is he has no references, no degrees, no education. Actually, this is no problem at all. Today, anyone can get an instant diploma from just about any educational institution or university. Your mail order diploma will even be watermarked, sealed, and signed for added authenticity. These diplomas are indistinguishable from the real thing. You can get degrees in the health and medical fields, from acupuncture to chiropractic to urine therapy and just about anything

The Internet is a gateway to fake identification and fake credentials. Many are good enough to fool professionals. This is why the informaton in paper credentials should always be verified.

between. The next time you go to a health practitioner, don't rely on the fancy diplomas on the wall. Check him (or her) out before being examined. Anyone can get diplomas and credentials ranging from certificates to Baccalaureate, Masters, or Ph.D.s, and even fake job references if need be . . . all sold for novelty purposes, of course.

Anyone who wants to disappear and reappear with a new identity, Social Security number, and driver's license can do so with the help of the Internet. Driver's licenses can be purchased for virtually every state. These are complete with holographs and magnetic stripes. These copies are hard to distinguish from the real thing. With a fake diploma and a fake driver's license in hand, whats else could one possibly need? How about a fake credit card and a Social Security card with your new name imprinted on them? This too is available on the Internet. Your cost to establish a new identity with four pieces of identification is about $200. Mind you, companies that offer these products or services do not advocate using them to purchase alcohol or commit other fraudulent activities. In fact, getting caught with fake identification can get you into a lot of trouble. Don't do it. Law enforcement agencies are getting wise, and penalties are getting stiffer. Some state laws prohibit the sale of fake IDs.

Besides being able to purchase IDs online, anyone with a computer and scanner can create or modify any piece of paper. Once anything is digitized (scanned into a computer), it can be manipulated, modified, and reprinted to look like the original. Any document can be changed easily, including driver's licenses, birth certificates, diplomas, Social Security cards, and anything else you can think of. The bottom line in today's digital world is that paper documents cannot be trusted. Verify the information with another source.

****

There will undoubtedly be critics of this book. People may not understand why this information needs to be brought into the mainstream. It needs to be brought into the mainstream so that parents and society can deal with it. We are, after all, a nation of laws. Parents, teachers, politicians, police officers, and lawmakers need to understand the new world of technology. We need to enforce existing laws, not contemplate censorship.

The Internet is an open communication forum where people around the world share and exchange information. Good and evil exist side by side on the Internet, like ebony and ivory on the keyboard. Parents and teachers should monitor computer activity closely to make the best of the Internet experience.

MISINFORMATION IN THE NEW WORLD

This book was written to give the reader an overview of issues relating to computers, computer security, investigation, privacy, privacy protection, and related resources.

We live in a world driven by digital information. It is estimated that 98 percent of all information is now stored in digital form. Computers and information processing ushered in an entirely new era of communications abilities. The amount of information at our disposal is growing exponentially, as is our ability to share information. Today's information age is filled with new opportunities for learning, education, and exploration. Few people, though, ever consider the dangers of the information age—dangers from intruders, eavesdroppers, spies, saboteurs, stalkers, and cons.

A final thought, however, should be given to some of the dangers of who controls information in this new era. First, we have to recognize that everyone wants to control, limit, distort, and cleanse information. This is a fundamental human characteristic. We all want our views to become public but want to limit the views of people with different opinions.

Many of the world's governments still exercise near total control over the media. This, of course, is done for propaganda purposes. Governments do not want their people to be exposed to other thoughts or different ideas and images. To control information, governments punish those who dare challenge the party line. In many parts of the world freedom of speech can be dangerous to your health: you can be killed for expressing other thoughts.

In free societies, like the United States, the government does not control information. In theory, at least, we have freedom of speech and freedom of the press. In reality, however, this is not the case. Our nation is moving toward having a media that is as restrained and restricted as that of repressive governments.

Ironically, the greatest threat to our freedom of speech and freedom of information comes not from the government. You won't find the U.S. army taking over the nation's television stations, radio stations, or publishers. You won't find government censors working side by side with reporters, limiting, changing, black-lining, cleansing. The means by which our media is being controlled are much more subtle. Few people even notice that it's taking place. The fact that there are no visible signs of a media takeover makes it very dangerous.

Ironically, the first attack against information and freedom of speech comes from the very people who, in theory, are supposed to protect our constitutional rights: lawyers. Legal action and threats of legal action are putting increasing pressures on the media and on publishers to limit, censor, cleanse, and otherwise restrict information. The aftermath of the *Hit Man* lawsuit against Paladin Press is one such instance. The book *Hit Man* is no longer available on the market because of a lawsuit against the publisher. The fact that Paladin's insurance company settled this case over the objections of the publisher will only spur other such lawsuits, each one testing new grounds, testing new works, pushing the envelope. This, of course, in hopes of receiving a hefty cash settlement.

The result of these legal attacks is that publishers and the media are increasingly jittery. As a result, they are limiting and restricting information based upon fear—fear of lawsuits. Fear . . . the very same emotion that all repressive governments use to limit what is printed. How is this situation different from the actions of a dictatorial government that threatens to take a reporter's property or liberty? In effect, it's no different. In both cases, information is restricted because of fear. The fear of lawsuits has created a severe self-censorship in our nation. Books are disappearing; information is being restricted, censored, cleansed. The result is that our freedom of speech, our freedom of the press, our freedom of self-expression has been terribly stifled.

Any information can be misused. The book *Hit Man* could be misused, as could any published work. Will the publisher of a book about target shooting be liable for the action of a criminal who uses that information to fine-tune his shooting skills to assassinate an elected official? What about fiction or true crime books? These books often spur copycat crimes. Will we hold the writer financially liable for someone who commits a copycat crime after reading a novel or watching a movie? This is already happening. Filmmaker Oliver Stone and Time Warner Entertainment Co. were sued in Louisiana on the grounds that the movie *Natural Born Killers* led a couple to shoot a woman during a robbery. In their lawsuit, the victim's family alleged that the movie inspired the shooting by glamorizing violence. Initially, the case was thrown out on First Amendment grounds. However, a Louisiana appeals court ruled that the movie was not protected by the First Amendment because the intent of the film's producers was at issue. The court ruled that the plaintiffs must have the opportunity to prove their case that Stone and Warner Entertainment made the film with the intention of inspiring viewers to go on murder sprees. Whatever the outcome, this lawsuit (which was ongoing as this book went to press) will certainly have a chilling effect on the types of movies that will be produced in the future. What about books about how to conduct homicide investigations? Can't they teach killers how to avoid mistakes and become better killers? I recently watched a television program about arson investigation. The program aired on an educational cable channel. The program explained in detail how an arsonist was able to set a fire and get away before it started. Anyone who watched this program could use that information to commit arson. If this should happen, will some lawyer sue the producer, the cable channel, and others associated with making or airing this program? I think you know the answer.

In the future, the increasing threat of legal action will create even more extreme pressure to cleanse, censor, and restrict access to information—not only printed information but that reported in any media, as well as online information. We are witnessing the beginning of an extremely dangerous trend, one that can have devastating consequences to our "free" society.

A second threat to freedom of information in the information age is a result of expanding corporate control of the media. Corporations and special interest groups are increasingly buying interests in the news media. They realize that by having a controlling interest in the media, they can exert their corporate muscle to limit, exclude, cleanse, restrict, and distort information. Remember, anyone can buy a newspaper; anyone can buy a book publishing company; anyone can buy a television station. Once they own it, they can ensure that their views are quietly foisted on the public. The fact that they also make money is the icing on the corporate cake.

Corporations have only one goal: they want you to open your wallet and spend, spend, spend. What happens, for example, when consumers feel insecure about the future? They won't spend. Thus a corporate-controlled media will tend to minimize any "negative" news. Corporations need to give us the feeling that all is well with the world.

Another alarming trend in the information age is a curious merging of news and commercials. I recently watched a national weather broadcast on which the announcer reported of a warming trend and suggested that viewers go to __MART to buy a fan. What's next? A news report about home invasions where a reporter suggests viewers buy a home security system? Will advertisers influence the kind of news that will be reported or aired in order to sell more of their products? The answer is yes; it's already happening. A magazine recently touted a new miracle cure: vinegar. This story was on the front page, right alongside a large picture of a bottle of name-brand vinegar. It is so much easier to sell advertising when one of your stories benefits a company's product. And selling advertising and making money often take precedent over accurate reporting.

We had better wake up to what's happening here. We are witnessing the beginning of a dangerous trend in information control by corporations. Once this influence and control is firmly entrenched, you will no longer be able to separate commercials from news and information.

The established media will always be subverted because it depends on advertising dollars. Advertisers influence what is reported in the news and what is shown over the public airwaves. The media cleverly slinks away from reporting anything advertisers find objectionable or controversial. If such stories are reported, they end up being so watered down that they are virtually useless. Advertisers routinely threaten to (and do) pull their commercials after negative news reports about their industry. A real estate group started its own advertising paper after the existing newspaper reported on news deemed "negative" to the sale of homes. It didn't matter that the story was accurate. As long as it cut down on the short-term sale of homes, reporting on such a story was a threat. The newspaper lost tons of advertising revenue. Others quickly took note. Do you think any newspaper would publish a report that uncovered the symbiotic relationship between home inspectors and the real estate agent? Absolutely not, because the agents would write angry letters in protest and pull their advertising to punish the paper, causing the paper to teeter on the verge of bankruptcy.

It is because of advertising sponsorships that you cannot rely on newspapers to report accurately on any number of important subjects. Papers play it safe by gently dancing around their advertisers. The result is that news is not reported based on its interest or importance, but rather on its acceptability to the advertisers.

I used to live in a city where one particular furniture store had several bogus "going out of business" sales at least three times within a few years. Each time the store "went out of business," the event was announced through tons of bold and expensive newspaper ads.

Part of this furniture store's campaign was to hire dozens of people who donned signs about the latest "going out of business sale." One day, the newspaper ran a regular "news story" about how this furniture store put dozens of sign carriers to work. I couldn't believe what I was reading. Here is a store that is obviously luring customers with deceptive advertising and bogus "sales." The newspaper knew what was going on here. Despite that, they ran a "news story" about how this company employed dozens of sign carriers. Give me a break! Mind you, this was not some backwater weekly; it was an established paper in a city with a population of more than 100,000. This is not an isolated incident! It happens all the time, and the trend is growing at an alarming pace.

The dangers of misinformation in the information age are further exacerbated by the fact that the Internet and the information age make it easy for corporations to distribute mountains of electronic press releases. These releases are written in corporate newspeak and are full of half-truths, distortions, and hype. Media releases, distributed with the help of the information superhighway, make it easy for overworked reporters to put together a "story." I recently watched a news report about "new research" that showed how successful weight-loss programs were. This particular segment looked like a news story; maybe it even fooled gullible reporters and producers eager for easy news. For me, however, it smelled of propaganda from the diet industry. News that is spawned by media releases is not objective and cannot be trusted.

Corporations and other special interests have become very clever in distributing information to the media, thereby controlling what you read, see, and hear. As a result, information that is really important, information that really matters, information that requires hard investigative work often goes by the wayside. It's much easier to take some media release and use it to write a story than to do a good investigative report.

Some time ago, I was surprised to see several lengthy messages on one of our local news stations railing against NATO's bombing of Yugoslavia. No equal time was given to anyone with another point of view. It was a completely one-sided propaganda statement in the true fashion of a Nazi propaganda machine. Is this what the news is all about? Is it a special privilege of those who own and control the public airwaves? It does not matter if you were for or against NATO's actions in Yugoslavia; the public needs balanced information. In theory, that is the purpose of the news. In reality, however, bias, distortion, selection, and weeding out have turned the media into a bedfellow of corporate and special interests.

Today we have access to more information than ever before. Yet increasingly this "information" cannot be trusted. Our society needs to develop a healthy distrust of the media. I am not implying that the Internet is any better. Misinformation on the Internet is rampant, but at least everyone has a chance to be heard. This same openness does not apply to other media and television.

If we want to build a better society in the information age, we need to be able to analyze information objectively, to separate truth from half-truths and half-truths from lies. We need to be able to tell the difference between information and commercials and corporate propaganda.

A society that is misinformed cannot make the right decisions. I am reminded of the Challenger space shuttle disaster. Engineers warned that it was too cold to proceed with a launch since the O-rings could fail in cold temperatures. Since the powers-that-be wanted a launch, reports of potential failure were downplayed and the launch proceeded. We all know what happened. Accurate information is crucial in a free society. Without it, we may ultimately self-destruct. Accurate information helps us make informed decisions. Our biased and distorted media does not help us make informed decisions.

Computers and technology now give us access to more information than ever before. Yet increasingly, this information cannot be trusted. If we are to survive and solve our problems, we need to teach ourselves and teach our kids how to think independently, critically, and objectively. We need to understand that the majority of information bombarding us is not designed to educate; it is designed to confuse and mislead.

Today, the Internet is one of the last bastions of free speech on the planet. Every step must be taken to ensure that the Internet remains a place where people can share information without restriction or limitation. This is not to say that information on the Internet can be trusted any more than any other source. Cons, fraud, deception, and rip-offs are probably more common on the Internet than they are anyplace else. But the Internet is the one medium that still offers a forum for open communication between people of the world. It's where you can communicate with anyone else on the planet and share your ideas, beliefs, and concerns. It's where your site can become as popular as any corporate site. It's where information, ideas, feelings of all varieties can be posted, expressed, disseminated, circulated, advocated, or opposed. It's an electronic bulletin board of free speech.

Computers in the information age have given us unprecedented new powers and opened modernistic vistas and possibilities. Computers and the Internet have also jeopardized our privacy and created a need to protect our kids from new dangers. Computers have created a new need to safeguard our information from the prying eyes or destructive efforts of others.

Computers, the Internet, and all the software in the world can't solve our problems. That's because information by itself is fruitless without a human mind to make sense of it, to understand it, to analyze it and learn how to apply it to make the world a better place.

RESOURCES

The following information is a list of resources for the software outlined in this book. Please remember that physical addresses and online addresses can change over time. In today's high-tech, fast-paced environment, companies can merge or change distributors. Their online addresses can change or be moved. Nothing is set in stone.

If you should experience difficulty with an address, please do not contact the publisher. In the event of a change, use a search engine to locate updated information.

AccessData Corporation
(Password recovery, more)
2500 North University Ave., Ste. 200
Provo, UT 84604-3864
http://www.accessdata.com

ANNA, Ltd.
(Stealth Keyboard Interceptor, HookProtect, PC Security Guard, more)
http://www.geocities.com/SiliconValley/Hills/8839
/products.html

ANCORT
(Security software, more)
http://www.ancort.ru/English/default.asp

ASR Data Acquisition & Analysis, LLC
(Expert Witness, more)
11422 Morning Glory Trail
Austin, TX 78750-1399
http://www.asrdata.com

Bonzi Software
(Internet ALERT '99)
http://www.bonzi.com

Carl's Electronics
(Voice stress analyzer plans)
P.O. Box 182
Sterling, MA 01564
http://www.electronickits.com

CODEX Data Systems
(D.I.R.T., more)
167 Route 304
Bardonia, NY 10954
http://www.thecodex.com/

CRAK Software
(Password recovery software)
814 E. Coral Gables Dr.
Phoenix, AZ 85022
http://www.crak.com

Cyber Detective
(Cyber Detective ToolKit)
http://cyberdetective.net

Cyber Spy
(Cyber Spy Toolkit)
http://cyber-spy.com

DEMCOM
(Steganos)
Hansmann/Wildgrube/Yoran GBR
Sophienst. 28
60487 Frankfurt, Germany
http://www.steganography.com/english/index.htm

Inso Corporation
(QuickView Plus, more)
31 St. James Ave.
Boston, MA 02116
http://www.inso.com

IPS CORP
(Triple Exposure, more)
2087F State Route 256
Reynoldsburg, OH 43068
http://www.ips-corp.com/

Language Force
(Universal Translator)
1601 East Lincoln Ave.
Orange, CA 92865
http://www.languageforce.com/

Mil-Spec Industries
(Truster, more)
10 Mineola Ave.
Roslyn Heights, NY 11577
http://www.mil-spec-industries.com/truster/index2.htm

NAIS
(PI Web Browser)
http://www.pimall.com/piweb/Default.htm

Network Associates, Inc.
(PGP Personal Privacy, more)
3965 Freedom Circle
Santa Clara, CA 95054
http://www.nai.com/

New Technologies, Inc
(MicroZap, DiskScrub, M-SWEEP, computer forensics)
2075 Northeast Division St.
Gresham, OR 97030
http://secure-data.com/intro.html

Omniquad Ltd.
(Desktop Surveillance, Detective, Mailwall, more)
Suite 1 Hanovia House
28/29 Eastman Road
London W3 7YG, UK
http://www.omniquad.com

PI Mall
(PI Scan, PI Web Browser, more)
http://www.pimall.com

Power Quest
(Lost & Found)
1359 N. Technology Way, Building K
Orem, UT 84097-2395
http://www.powerquest.com/

Privacy Software Corporation
(NS Clean, IE Clean, more)
http://www.privsoft.com/

Softseek
(Mutilate, File Wiper, PC Activity Monitor, more)
http://softseek.com/Utilities/File_Management_and_Searching/Revi
ew_10769_index.html

SoftwareSolutions.net
(Who's Talking)
SSNet, Inc.
240 S. Broadway, Ste. 101
Denver, CO 80209-1564
http://softwaresolutions.net/index.htm

Symantec
(Norton Utilities, Your Eyes Only)
http://www.symantec.com

Tropical Software
(PC Security, Stealth Encyrptor, more)
704 228th Ave. NE, Ste. 103
Redmond, WA 98053
http://www.tropsoft.com

Trustech, Ltd.
(Truster, more)
Makh-Shevet House
28 Arlozorov St.
46448 Herzelia, Israel
http://www.truster.com/

Verity, Inc.
(KeyView, Pro)
894 Ross Dr.
Sunnyvale, CA 94089
http://www.keyview.com/